FULLY YOU

Unlocking the Power of
All You Really Are

FULLY YOU

Unlocking the
Power of All
You Really Are

JOËL MALM

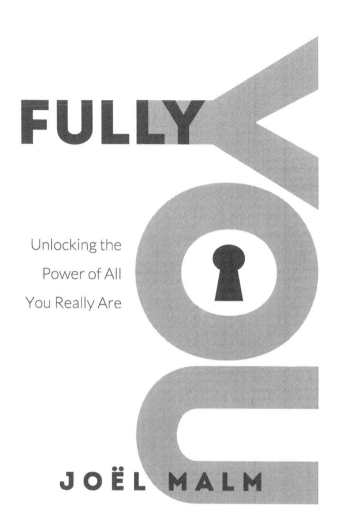

MGPRESS

FULLY YOU: UNLOCKING THE POWER OF ALL YOU REALLY ARE

ISBN-13: 978-0-9985085-2-8

Cover design and layout by Five J's Design

Published in the United States by MG Press.

ACKNOWLEDGEMENTS

This book would not have been possible without the ongoing input and research of David F. Allen, MD. His work is the foundation for much of what is shared in this book.

Dedicated to Emily and Elise.
You are the most unexpected joys of my life.

CONTENTS

CHAPTER 1

HIDING THE REAL YOU

Most men lead lives of quiet desperation....

—HENRY DAVID THOREAU

We live life wounded.

Most of us don't walk around feeling wounded. What we feel are the effects of being wounded: we feel insecurity, loneliness, resentment, and discouragement.

We want to embrace life to the fullest, be true to who we really are, to give and receive love. But too often that feels just beyond our grasp. But we've got just enough hope in us to keep going. We read self-help books, go to seminars, listen to sermons, pray, and white-knuckle it, believing that if we just try a little harder we'll find the abundant life we know is out there. But we can never seem to find it, and are left wondering...

Is this the best I can do?

The sad truth is, this is the point where most people give up. They get tired of trying so hard and they just settle. They accept a life that falls far short of what God has for them. But here's the thing: this all happens because we've believed a lie. A series of lies, actually. Lies we were told before we knew any better. And based on those lies, we inadvertently developed a false self. A person your Creator never intended for you to be. That false self convinces us to hide behind a mask, to never put ourselves out there, to play it safe, and to be who we think people want us to be. We get really good at playing this role. It becomes safe and familiar. But it can become an exhausting game. One that holds us back from being who we truly can be.

I'm familiar with this exhausting game, because I spent many years of my life living this way. Depending on how well I performed, I flip-flopped between loving and loathing myself. I knew exactly what to say to impress people. I worked hard to craft an image of invincibility, but I was insecure and hypersensitive to criticism. I tried to be perfect so no one could embarrass me by correcting me. I was the king of control. But just below the surface?

I was full of depression and anger. I still managed to get a lot done. I got a college degree. I worked for a Fortune 500 company. I even managed to start a backpacking organization taking people all over the world on outdoor adventures. My book *Vision Map* is about starting that organization and about pursuing the dreams in your heart. But this book is about what happens next.

Because here's how it usually goes down.

You get what you wanted. God makes the dream come true—you get the guy (or gal), you start the business, you have the baby, you get your first ministry job, you make your first million. But then you realize that getting it wasn't the hardest part. Not messing it up once you have it is the hardest part. You are still you, and all your anxiety, self-image issues, insecurity, perfectionism, and anger—all that stuff you've been ignoring—threatens to undermine the very thing you worked so hard to get.

Look around and you'll see lots of people sabotaging the very thing they wanted. Your sister married a wonderful man and raised some great kids, but in her mid-thirties she got obsessed with body image and ditched her family for a twenty-two-year-old personal trainer. Your pastor was an amazing leader and Bible teacher, but he was forced to re-sign when his pornography addiction was discovered. Your college roommate married a great woman, but lost her because he has anger issues. The guy down the street made tons of money, but gambled it all away and got his house foreclosed on. And if you're honest about it, you realize that could happen to you too. In moments of clarity and authenticity you know you need to do something about your issues.

But…well…*everyone's* got issues. So you just keep pushing them away, ignore them, and hope they'll work themselves out. All the while living in fear of losing everything you have and working harder to try to keep it. Or you may just end up feeling stuck and find yourself asking, *Why is this happening again?*

Problems don't go away.

Ignoring our issues won't make them any better. We may get everything we think we wanted, but if we don't deal with our deeper issues we can easily lose what we worked so hard to get. Or worse, we could spend our entire life living in fear and anxiety, far short of what God wants for us.

We have to face our issues.

I had a laundry list of issues, but over a one-year period, while backpacking around the world from the jungles of Central America to the basecamp of Mt. Everest, that began to change. They didn't go away overnight. Sometimes I still struggle with them. But I began a journey through a series of deep truths that changed everything for me. Those truths led me to get a master's degree in counseling so I could help others find the freedom I'd found.

But after getting that master's degree I had another realization: I don't like counseling. I don't like wallowing in the past. I like action. I like forward movement. So, I started doing personal development coaching, helping people reach their potential. Forget the past, let's move forward!

And then I discovered what I just talked about. Most of us have a general idea where we want to be, but we have mental barriers, faulty beliefs, and general dysfunction that stop us dead in our tracks. Our issues undermine our forward movement. So where do these issues come from?

Lots of places. We inherited some beliefs and patterns from parents, teachers, and pastors who told us what we should believe about ourselves, all based on what they believe about themselves. We had no reason to question those beliefs, so we just went with them. Other beliefs came from the bumps and bruises we got along the way. Life rumbled along—we graduated, had kids, got the dream job—but all the while something was building just below the surface within us. And before we realize it, we start to feel the symptoms of the wounds.

One day we break into tears at work. Or we find ourselves regularly driving around town, trying to blow off steam. We end up on a counselor's couch, or we just walk around in a perpetual state of grouchiness.

Too many people settle for this kind of living, and that is tragic. Because there is way more out there. There's an amazing life full of love and joy and peace. You don't have time to operate at half capacity because you're offended and depressed. There's too much adventure out there for you to miss out on it because you are afraid of what people think. You have people who love you and look up to you. You've got something to give this world and we don't have time for you to be anything short of who you really are—we need the unique gifts and abilities you bring to this world!

So this is a book about moving forward. It's about addressing the uncomfortable realities of the lies we've believed. It involves looking back and identifying where things got off track. But don't worry. We won't stay there for long. I'll show you a specific game plan to deal with the bad programming that is limiting you. A game plan based on the powerful truths I learned on my journey through Asia. I'm still learning how powerful all these truths are, they unfold in layers. But I write in hopes that, as you learn them, you will unlock everything that God placed within you and become who he says you can be.

JUST BE YOU

I started leading four-month backpacking trips around the world right out of college. I had no idea what I was doing. So I copied another program I admired. One month into my first trip I was exhausted. I hated what I had created. It didn't fit my personality. My insecurity flared up and I started questioning if I was the right person to be doing this. I was certain I was going to ruin everything.

A few weeks into the trip, we did a five-day hike through the mountains of western Guatemala, taking the Jesus Film to remote indigenous villages. A good friend of mine was on the team and knew I was discouraged. At one point on the trail he turned to me and said, "Joël, you know I came on this trip because I believe in you. Just be you. That's who we like."

I remember thinking, *Pfft! I can't just be me. Being me always gets me into trouble. No one likes that person.*

My thoughts flashed back to third-grade in Texas. I attended a strict religious school run by a stern, bearded man named Mr. Darby. He seemed determined to make it clear to us spirited third graders that life was a serious matter, full of obligation and duty and minimal amounts of joy. I'm pretty sure I never once saw that man smile.

Every Tuesday and Thursday our class would line up in a strict formation and head to the room next door for choir practice. Two times a year we performed at the Sunday morning service of the church that sponsored the school. We were all required to attend. This was a major problem for me, because my dad was a pastor at a church across town. (Yes, I'm a pastor's kid. That explains a lot, I know.) The Sunday of the concert my parents told me they were just too busy with church obligations to take me to the choir concert. My heart sank. I knew Mr. Darby was going to make me pay for not showing up.

The following day, right after lunch, Darby announced that we'd be forgoing our regular class for a party celebrating a successful choir concert. Giant smiles were shared around the room. He instructed us to line up. I assumed my place in the line, amazed I had escaped his wrath for not being there. But just as we were about to walk out of the room Darby called out my name.

"Joël, you won't be participating in the party since you chose to not show up yesterday. We can't reward someone who didn't participate." He pointed at my desk. In front of the entire class I lowered my head and walked to my desk. For the next hour I sat listening to the party next door.

Sitting there I concluded there was something wrong with my family and, by extension, there was something wrong with me. We were not normal. All those other kids made it to the concert. Their parents got them where they were supposed to be. But not me. My family was weird. I'd been humiliated because we were different—and because something was wrong with me.

Ok, you can wipe the tears from your eyes, I'm fine now. Really. But, here's what I know about you: You have a story like mine.

As you read that story did your mind flash back to a similar moment? Did you remember a moment early in your life when you first began to believe there was something wrong with you or your family? I have yet to meet a person who, with a little thought, can't recall a similar experience. Those kinds of experiences leave a mark. If you spend a few more minutes thinking back, other memories with a similar theme may come to mind. Those memories send you consistent messages. They create loops that shape what you believe about yourself and the world around you. All it takes is the right trigger and the loop starts playing.

I heard a story about a lady who walked past a beautiful parrot in a pet store. The parrot squawked. "Hey lady." The woman turned and smiled at the parrot. The parrot said, "Lady, you are ugly!"

Furious, the woman stormed to the counter and complained to the owner, who apologized profusely and promised it wouldn't happen again.

The storeowner went over, yanked the parrot from his cage by the neck. Feathers flew. He told the bird, "If you ever call that lady ugly again I will ring your neck." The parrot was traumatized.

Several days later the same woman walked into the store. She eyed the parrot, but wouldn't look at him directly. The parrot looked back and ducked his head. As the lady walked past, the parrot whispered. "Hey lady."

She whipped around. "What?"

The parrot grinned. "You know."

We all have our own little parrot talking to us. That annoying, squawking voice that says a thousand things:

"You'll never be good enough."

"If people really knew you and what you are they'd run."

"You are unlovable."

"You are a failure."

"There's something wrong with your family."

"You are a fraud and have no business in the position you hold."

"What would people think if you told them what you really thought?"

"You have no right to help others when you are so messed up."

We've heard our messages so many times that it doesn't even have to be said anymore. One wrong look from someone, an off-handed comment, a mistake we make, and the parrot in our head says, "You know."

Those words may have actually been spoken to you by a friend or family member, or the voice may be your personal explanation for the cards life has handed you. But either way the voice is always there.

That voice is shame.

We know how it feels to do something wrong and regret it. That's guilt. Guilt says, *You did something wrong.* But shame is deeper. Worse. Shame says, *There is something wrong with you.*

Now here's the deal. Apart from Jesus something *is* wrong with us. We've got a sin problem. But Jesus came and conquered the power of sin. So that shame voice should no longer have power over us, because "if anyone is in Christ, he is a new creation."[1] If you've received God's gift of salvation, there is a new person—the true you—deep inside. Recognizing this truth is the foundation for becoming fully you. When we surrender to God we get a new identity.

The problem is, we've spent a lifetime learning how to protect ourselves and hide from shame. God says we are new in Christ, but we have to unlearn a lifetime of old programing. That's what this book is about. Unlearning the old way and embracing who you really are, right now, in Christ.

God says we are new in Christ, but we have to unlearn a lifetime of old programing.

So let's see who God says you are. And who you aren't. Because your fear, insecurity, anger, limiting mindsets, bad habits, and defense mechanisms are no longer part of your true identity. You can stop holding on to them now. It's time to trade that false self in for your new identity rooted in courage, love, joy, peace, discipline, and truth.

If you are ready to begin the journey to becoming all God says you really are, then turn the page and join me on an adventure that starts in the wildest parts of Asia.

CHAPTER 2

THE HURT TRIANGLE

Shame, depart, thou art an enemy to my salvation.

—JOHN BUNYAN

The first clue that we had boarded the wrong

train came from the strange look we got from the young Chinese girl in a stiffly pressed blue uniform who was punching a hole in our tickets. She spoke no English, and though she smiled, she seemed shocked to have foreigners on her train.

As we rumbled along the tracks on the outskirts of Shenzhen, China, one of my team members leaned toward me. "Are you sure this is the right train, Joël?"

I looked at my small team. We'd be traveling together for the next four months, crossing China from the far south, heading up north into Mongolia, and ultimately on to Mt. Everest in Tibet. We'd spent the first few days of our trip in Hong Kong, smuggling Bibles, which the communist government had deemed illegal, into China. Now we were headed north for the next leg of our journey. But I had to admit…

It seemed we may have made a huge mistake.

Our tickets indicated in English that we were heading to Beijing. But something seemed off. There were no other foreigners on this train. So, I decided to do some investigating. Surely, I could find another group of backpackers who spoke a language I spoke. I walked through one cigarette-smoke-filled car after another—no one could help me.

When I reached the food car, a young girl apparently realized she had a chance to practice her English and came over to talk to me. When I showed her my tickets her eyes widened. The good news? We were indeed going to Beijing. The bad news? Apparently two trains left for Beijing at the same time. One was a K train, the other a T train. The T train was the express train that tourists took. My team and I had boarded the K train—the slow train—with the locals. This train stopped in every little village between Hong Kong and Beijing. What was supposed to be a twenty-hour journey was going to take us nearly two days!

I went back and told the team the news. There was a collective groan, but after we resigned ourselves to a long trip we all settled into our little nooks on the train and prepared for the ride ahead.

Looking back, I'm grateful we boarded the wrong train. That chugging train to Beijing was the first time in years I had been forced to slow down. During college I worked forty hours per week and took between fifteen and twenty-one hours of classes. I played in two bands. I cared for my grandfather, who lived an hour away. I even had a girlfriend for a while.

As soon as I graduated I started leading teams around the world. We started in Central America. Now we were in Asia. I loved being on the move and packed my schedule full. I was going 24/7…until that train ride.

Which brings up a really important point to start with. If you want to really make some changes in your life, at some point you're going to have to slow down. You'll have to create some space to evaluate your life. It probably won't just happen. Life always creeps in and keeps us busy. You'll have to make the time. We'll talk about that more later in the book. But for now, know that if nothing changes, nothing changes. To bring

If nothing changes, nothing changes.

lasting change you'll have to be willing to slow down, take a step back, and look around.

My change started during that slow ride. On that ride I met Dr. David Allen. Or at least I felt like I did as I read his book. A few weeks earlier, a friend suggested I read one of his books.[1] What my friend shared from that book was so intriguing that I ordered it on Amazon and it arrived just before our flight to Asia.

I started reading it on that train ride, and I couldn't put it down.

Dr. Allen started by explaining that every human is born with three basic instinctual needs: Safety, Connection, and Empowerment.

We all need to feel safe. We are born completely helpless and look to our parents and other adults to give us protection. That need never goes away. Throughout our lives we do whatever we can to establish safety and security for ourselves and our family.

We all need to feel a connection to others. We need affection and esteem from people around us. We want to feel valued and accepted. As we grow, this need doesn't go away. In many ways, as we mature emotionally we have even greater need for connection.

We all need to feel empowered. We need to feel we have some say over our lives, some autonomy. We want to exert our will, to feel we can make our own choices.

These three needs create a "triangle of needs" like the one below.

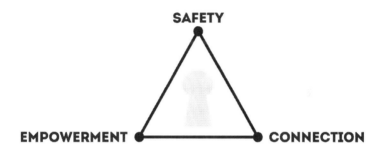

In the Garden of Eden, we had all this and more. God gave Adam and Eve everything they needed. With no sin in the world they were safe and secure. They had a perfect connection with God. So much so that God actually came and walked with them in the evenings. God empowered them and gave them total freedom to make their own decisions. They had it made. "Adam and his wife were both naked, and they felt no shame."[2] Nothing to hide, nothing to fear. No shame.

The moment Adam and Eve chose sin, things got messy: "Then the eyes of both of them were opened, and they realized they were naked; so they sewed fig leaves together and made coverings for themselves." Shame exploded on the scene and they immediately felt vulnerable and afraid. So they hid.

We've all been hiding ever since. We're trying to cover up an instinct that says we aren't what we should be. Philosophers call it *existential guilt.* Theologians call it *original sin.* Whatever you call it, we all feel it. It's the voice of that parrot. It's shame. It's a vulnerable feeling that makes us want to hide.

After Adam's and Eve's eyes were opened, the Lord came looking to spend time with Adam and asked, "Where are you?"

Adam responded by admitting his shame. "I heard you in the garden, and I was afraid because I was naked; so I hid." [3] Brené Brown has spent years studying shame. In one survey she asked participants to describe what vulnerability feels like. The word that most participants used was *Naked.* [4] Shame feels like nakedness. It makes us want to hide.

Shame comes from lots of places. It can come from being a victim of abuse, divorce, our own addictions and the addictions of others, physical deformities, excessive weight, where you lived growing up, and family history. And that's just a start to a long list. If you want to hide it or keep it a secret, it's probably based in shame. One young woman shared with me how much shame she felt that her parents had entered the United States ille-gally. She always tried to hide her heritage. She refused to learn her parents' native language, hoping to wipe away the feelings she had about her family history.

> *If you want to hide it or keep it a secret, it's probably based in shame.*

I feel shame and insecurity whenever I walk into a car parts store and don't know what the part I need looks like. I'm just certain the guys behind the counter are laughing at me as some white-collar hack who thinks he can fix cars. And it goes the other way. A friend of mine who works a blue-collar job (and is one of the smartest guys I know) told me he gets insecure around white-collar guys, "They make money with their minds. I have to get dirty to make money."

Women feel shame and insecurity around other wom-en who seem to have it all together and keep everything perfect all the time. We all feel shame.

When we don't get one of our three basic needs met we feel shame in three specific areas. When we don't get safety, we feel shame as abandonment. When we don't get connection, we feel rejection. When we don't get empowerment, we feel humiliation. This is called the *Hurt Triangle.* And it affects our lives in ways we may have never realized.

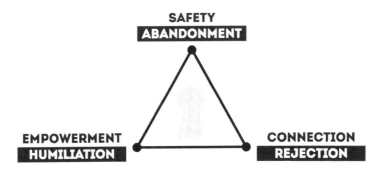

WHERE THE PAIN REALLY STARTS

One of the most popular hikes I lead is a four-day trek through the Andes Mountains of Southern Peru. On the fourth day, we hike into the ancient Inca fortress of Machu Picchu, one of the Seven Wonders of the World.

I've done the hike several times and it's very challenging, but I know how to prepare and rarely have problems. But last year, halfway through the trip, I started getting sharp pains in my right knee. I was immediately concerned. I worried that maybe after years of hiking I had seriously injured my knee. Was my hiking career over?

I made it through the hike despite quite a bit of pain. I hoped the pain would go away once I took a break and rested, but it continued even after I got home. It flared up when I would walk up or down any small step. While visiting my family, I mentioned to my physical therapist sister-in-law that I was having knee pain, so she started quizzing me about it.

"Where does it hurt exactly?"

I pointed to the place. "There, just below the knee cap."

She bent down and pushed on the spot. "Does this hurt?" She pushed on several spots, asking the same question. Some places hurt, others didn't. After about a minute of poking she stood up. "You have weak hips."

What? "But, my hips don't hurt. It's my knee."

"Nope. It's your hips. Your knee has to compensate for your weak hips. Make your hips stronger and the knee pain will go away."

She showed me some exercises and told me to start doing them every day. I was sure she was wrong, but I figured it couldn't hurt, so I did the exercises.

One week later the knee pain was gone! It was unbelievable. My knee *had* been compensating for my hips. My body helped me endure the pain during that hike, but the only way the pain went away was if I got all of my body working the way it should.

Our emotions and thoughts also compensate when we are hurt and feel shame. We develop emotional defense mechanisms. Unfortunately, just like my knee, the problem doesn't go away if you don't deal with the real source. It just comes out as pain in another area.

THE GREAT WALL

When we feel shame, we make an inner vow, telling ourselves—usually subconsciously—that we'll never let that happen again.

"No one will ever hurt me that way again."

"I'll never give someone that much of my heart again."

"No one will ever leave me alone and helpless again."

The moment we make our inner vow, we start to build a line of defense against being hurt again. We start to build a wall. A façade. A false self.

Each area of shame has a specific defense mechanism.

RESPONDING TO ABANDONMENT

When we don't get the safety we need, we feel abandoned. We respond with a defense mechanism of self-absorption. If no one is going to look out for us, we'll look out for our self. Abandonment leaves us feeling inadequate, driven by a fear that we aren't enough—smart enough, lovable enough, good-looking enough—you fill in the blank. We believe the lie that if we had been enough that person wouldn't have left. A CEO of a large company told me about a time his parents got mad at him and said, "We're leaving and never coming back!" They weren't serious, but he didn't know that. They left and came back an hour later, but for that entire hour he believed his parents had left him. That one experience left a mark. Fighting his fear of abandonment drove him to succeed. But it also drove him to self-absorption, which led to isolation and loneliness. He had everything, and he was miserable.

When someone we look to for safety leaves us we feel alone and vulnerable, so we do whatever it takes to protect ourselves. We ignore the needs and concerns of those around us, believing that we have bigger challenges than them. Our life is more important than the life of anyone around us. We may never say that, but we act this way. Our schedule, our needs, our priorities are most important. We've all got a little bit of this in us. But for those hurt in the area of abandonment it's more pronounced.

The extreme version of this self-absorption is narcissism, which is a mental illness. Narcissists have little empathy for others. They exploit and use people. They believe the rules don't apply to them. They believe they are special and can only relate to certain groups of people. They seem strong and charming, but just below the surface they feel inadequate and insecure. They are very fragile. But they rarely show weakness, because they fear it will lead to them being abandoned again.

Self-absorption creates the illusion of safety, but it actually leads to isolation.

RESPONDING TO REJECTION

When we don't feel accepted by those around us, we feel rejected. Rejection doesn't necessarily have to be overt, someone telling us, "We don't like you." It's often subtler than that. It's parents comparing siblings: "Why can't you be more like your sister?" It's someone in your life who always raises the bar and makes you feel like you can never get their approval. It's feeling like an outsider because of where you came from or how you were raised.

When people feel an ongoing lack of approval from those around them, they tend to go one of two ways. Some try harder. They go overboard pleasing people and seeking their approval. Being liked, online or in person, becomes an obsession. Others just choose to give up on relationships at the first sign of rejection. One man in his sixties told me he never really felt like he had a problem with rejection because he had become so good at rejecting others at the first sign of them not accepting him.

When we feel rejected we respond with a defense mechanism of self-gratification. We've all got a little bit of this defense mechanism in us. Our subconscious says, "People may reject me, but food, or sex, or drugs, or physical fitness, or masturbation, or pornography will always be there for me." These things become our silent companion. They offer ongoing connection. But they are just an illusion of connection. A cheap substitute.

A trademark of self-gratification is swapping one obsession for another. You know these folks. They go "all-in" with a diet or exercise regimen, then just a few weeks later you find they've moved on and are preaching to you about a new obsession you need to know about. "Paleo, bro. Go paleo!" They are obsessed with finding one high after another. Overeating, overspending, over exercising—anything that brings an immediate good feeling or rush.

When those obsessions become all-consuming they can turn into addiction. Dr. Bruce Alexander has studied addiction for years, and he believes it is often directly linked to a lack of connection, real or perceived, in the addict's life. Some of his research is controversial, but it's definitely food for thought.

Early in his career, Dr. Alexander watched a U.S. government sponsored anti-drug campaign that showed a rat in a cage drinking from a water bottle that contained cocaine. The voice over the commercial said, "Only one drug is so addictive, nine out of ten laboratory rats will use it. And use it. And use it. Until dead. It's called cocaine. And it can do the same thing to you." A rat is shown running around frantically until he drops dead. The commercial was an attempt to slow the cocaine epidemic ravaging America in the 1980s.

Dr. Alexander noticed that the rats in these experiments were isolated and alone in their cages. He decided to adjust the experiment. He kept some rats isolated. But he put a bunch of rats together in a cage filled with lots of colored balls and running wheels—a rat paradise. He gave both groups, the isolated rats and the ones in the group, access to morphine—a highly addictive drug. The rats who were isolated used up to 25 milligrams of morphine per day. They clearly had an addiction. But the rats in a group hardly used any. Dr. Alexander reworked the experiment in lots of different ways and concluded that:

"Today's flood of addiction is occurring because our hyper-individualistic, frantic, crisis-ridden society makes people feel socially or culturally isolated. Chronic isolation causes people to look for relief. They find temporary relief in addiction to drugs or any other of a thousand habits and pursuits because it allows them to escape their feelings, to deaden their senses—and to experience an addictive lifestyle as a substitute for a full life."[5]

Interestingly, during that same decade, Dr. David Allen was working in Washington D.C. on fighting the cocaine epidemic. He came to a similar conclusion: There is a definite correlation between addiction and lack of connection in peoples' lives.

RESPONDING TO LACK OF EMPOWERMENT

When you feel a lack of empowerment you respond with a defense mechanism of perfectionism and control. Feeling powerless can be humiliating. If you grew up in a highly-controlled environment, with strict rules and limited freedom, there's a good chance you'll struggle in this area. I do. This is my corner of the triangle. The subconscious drive within me says *If I can be perfect, no one will ever embarrass or humiliate me.*

Interestingly, on the other side of the spectrum, folks who grew up with no structure and total freedom often respond in the same way, seeking to bring some order and control to their life.

My parents were never overly strict, but the Christian schools I attended were. Adding to that pressure was the fact that I was a pastor's kid living under constant scrutiny. There were spoken and unspoken expectations from those around me. I'll never forget a woman scolding me after I accidentally bumped into one of her children. "And you're a pastor's kid! You should be ashamed of yourself." People whose parents are in positions of power or influence regularly tell me they felt the same pressure. They were told that they were a direct representation of their parents, "So don't mess up!" Talk about pressure. Trying to be perfect is an attempt to bring a sense of control and avoid embarrassment. But being perfect is an impossible standard.

Perfectionism can keep you from either starting new projects or finishing what you start. You never start the book because you are afraid it won't be perfect on the first shot. Your house turns into one endless remodeling project because, in your mind, it's never the way it needs to be. Doing things right and well is one thing, but perfectionism can bring you to a screeching standstill. *Perfect* is the enemy of *done*. Many people never step out into a new calling because they aren't sure they'll be able to meet their own standards. Obsession with control can keep you from moving forward.

The extreme version of this desire for control is Obsessive Compulsive Disorder. I hear people joke about having OCD all the time, but for folks who really have it, it's not fun. It's overwhelming. Life feels like it's always out of control.

PUTTING IT ALL TOGETHER

Put all the needs, hurts, and defenses together and it looks like this:

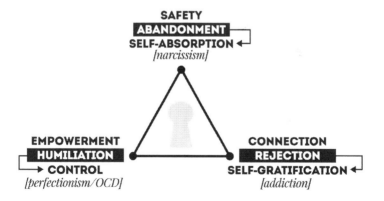

When I explain the hurt triangle to a group of people, someone almost always blurts out, "Oh! That's my brother!", or husband, or mother. It's easy to see another person's dysfunction and how it's actually repelling love and keeping them from what they really want. But this book is about *you* becoming who God says you really are, and to do that you need to recognize what defenses are holding *you* back. As Socrates said, "The unexamined life is not worth living."

If we want to be all God wants us to be the question we need to ask is, "What defenses have I developed that are keeping me from being free to love and be loved?"

If we want to be all God wants us to be the question we need to ask is, "What defenses have I developed that are keeping me from being free to love and be loved?"

King Solomon said, "The purpose in a man's heart is like deep water, but a man of understanding will draw it out."[6]

You and I are deep people. Our thoughts, feelings, and actions all start from a deep place within us. What we see on the outside (behaviors) are a direct result of what's going on inside (beliefs). Our job is to draw out and explore what shame-based beliefs are limiting us. We have to identify the beliefs we have about ourselves that conflict with who God says we are in Christ. The problem is, we are too close to our problems and defenses to even recognize them. Defenses can become so engrained that we don't see them for what they are. Instead, we believe they are who we are. But they aren't. There is a deeper, truer version of you that has been hiding.

The secret to unlocking that hidden part of you starts with exploring something we are all familiar with: anger and frustration.

Just a few days before that train ride to Beijing I had learned a life-changing truth about anger. When I put that together with what I learned about our basic needs and shame, it helped me see that anger can be a power for good. So what was that truth about anger?

For that, we have to go back to Hong Kong, where my friends and I were smuggling contraband.

CHAPTER 3

THE GIFT OF ANGER

If you've ever met a man, then you've met an angry man.

— DAN ALLENDER

Hong Kong International Airport is an example of what humankind is capable of if they get desperate enough.

Up until 1998, Hong Kong's main airport was located right in the heart of that bustling city. Planes would rumble past the giant skyscrapers, shaking buildings and creating quite a scare for passengers who were unfamiliar with the airport's landing pattern. As Hong Kong grew, more and more flights started arriving. They knew they needed a new airport, but the tiny, mountainous island had no more space.

They decided to take some extraordinary measures. They completely leveled two entire mountains and moved all that land into the ocean. They built a 3.5 square mile island!

When I think about that epic accomplishment, I can't help but think of Jesus' words in Matthew 17:20, where he says, "if you have faith like a grain of mustard seed, you will say to this mountain, 'Move from here to there,' and it will move, and nothing will be impossible for you." Little did I realize when I landed on that airport island, a major mountain that had been in my life for years was about to get moved.

We based our smuggling operation in Hong Kong and entered mainland China each day, bringing Bible-based resources, which were illegal under the communist government. It was all cloak-and-dagger, with fake-bottom suitcases, Christian contraband, and secret rendezvous. We'd cross the border checkpoint in pairs to avoid drawing attention. Once we had a big enough cache of contraband we'd call a guy. A few minutes later, he'd pull up in his little nondescript car, we'd exchange a quick handshake, load the trunk, and he'd be on his way. We did this once in the morning and once in the evening.

You need a visa to enter China —not the credit card, the kind of visa that allows you permission to enter a country for a certain amount of time. At the time of our trip you were only allowed a double-entry visa—meaning you could only enter the country twice on one visa—so I had to get a new visa every day. Each double-entry visa cost $150. I hadn't expected this expense, and by the third afternoon in Hong Kong my budget was taking a serious hit.

Financial supporters gave every month to allow me to lead these mission teams. So I logged on to see how much money had been given to my account. The balance was low. The main church that had committed to support me had not sent in a gift that month, and that was one-third of my support. I started freaking out. I called my dad on the other side of the world to get his advice. It was early morning for him. We talked a little bit, and I decided that I would write the pastor the next day and mention what had happened. I had a short conversation with my mom to just say hi, then hung up and went to bed.

The next morning, as I was logging in to write my letter to the church, I received an email from the Missions Pastor at that church. His email made my stomach churn.

> *Hi Joel,*
>
> *Your mom called. She told us we forgot to send your support check. So sorry, I'll get that taken care of.*

I felt my face getting red. I slammed my hand down on the desk. *What was she thinking?!* I was a grown man whose mom had just contacted a supporting church, for goodness sake! It looked like I sent my mom to do something I was too afraid to do.

I stormed out of our little Hong Kong apartment and into a nearby park. Several middle-aged women were doing a peaceful Tai Chi routine outside, with Chinese Erhu violin music playing. It should have been a calm scene, but I was raging. I tried to calm down. *Why is this making me so angry? Mom was just trying to help.* After about 1.7 seconds of deep thought I couldn't get any clarity, so I gave up. I just knew I was angry. I decided I'd call her and give her a piece of my mind, no matter what time it was back home.

On my way to berate my poor mother I ran into Ellen, one of the missionaries who lived at the complex. A few days earlier I had discovered she was a counselor, so in passing I sarcastically said. "Hey. You're a counselor, right? Wanna help me with a mother problem?"

Her face lit up. "Sure. What's going on?"

Ellen actually seemed to care, so I started ranting about what my mom had done. She cocked her head and gave an understanding nod. "Wanna come up to our apartment for some tea?"

A few minutes later I was sitting in her living room. Her husband made us some tea. Once we were settled, tea in hand, she asked the classic therapist question. "So how do you feel about what your mom did?"

Pfft! That was easy. "I'm angry."

Ellen smiled. "Sure, you are angry. But what do you *really* feel? Anger is a secondary response. How did what she did make you feel?"

Ugh. Here we go. "Angry. Furious. Enraged. What are you looking for here?"

She smiled. "Well, I'm sure the anger came pretty quickly. But anger is always in response to something. So, what was the feeling just before anger?"

Now, I think it's important to stop here and admit something: I'd had an anger problem pretty much my entire life. I wouldn't have admitted that to anyone because back then I thought explosive anger was normal. In my mind, it really wasn't *my* problem, it was the people who were making me angry. I'd say things like, "If people didn't do such dumb things, I'd be fine! Can I help it if I respond when people do things I don't like?" And respond I did.

I'd say horrible, mean things only to regret them later. I'd break things and feel guilty about it. Some dear friends of mine regularly remind me that the first time we met they had just watched me throw drumsticks across a conference room because I was mad about the sound not being right for our band. I always cringe when they bring that story up. Not my finest moment...

Okay, back to the counseling session.

Things were getting uncomfortable on that couch. My mom was clearly the problem, *not* my emotions. This conversation was going nowhere. But Ellen insisted and she *had* made me tea, so I gave it some more thought. *What was I feeling right before I got angry? Hmm.* After a few moments I knew what it was, but I didn't want to admit it. I hesitated, but then surrendered. After all, if you can't be honest with a counselor, who can you be honest with? "I felt embarrassed. I'm a grown man whose mom is calling people for him."

Ellen nodded once. "There you go. You got it. You were embarrassed."

Which brings us to the most important thing you need to understand if you want to get anger working for you, rather than messing up your life: Anger is a secondary emotion.

Anger is always a response to another emotion. It's a signal that lets us know we need to pay attention and address a deeper problem.

A VITAL ENERGY

The Mandarin Chinese word for anger is shēng qì. (pronounced, *shung chee)* What's interesting is, the two Chinese characters that make up the word (生气) actually have their own separate meanings. *Shēng* means *to give birth. Qì* means *air* or a vague type of vital energy.[1] Put them together and you've got an insightful definition of anger: To give

Anger is a secondary emotion.

birth to vital energy. Anger drives us to respond. How we respond is what determines whether our anger will be productive or destructive.

When used correctly, anger is a gift that can help us look a little deeper into ourselves. When we're angry it's because we feel something we value is being threatened. Typically, when we get angry it's because we feel a threat to our safety, connection, or empowerment. Anger and the Hurt Triangle go hand-in-glove.

Now, before we proceed, let me address all you folks out there who say, "But I don't really get angry." That's fine for now. You can believe that. But don't skip this chapter. There's still something important you can get out of it. So if you believe you don't get angry, throughout this chapter, just replace the word *angry* with the words *frustrated* or *annoyed.* And hang with me. We'll talk later about the subtle forms of anger that don't seem like anger.

THE POWER OF ANGER

There are 1,189 chapters in the Bible. Anger shows up by chapter four. Anger kicked in right after Adam and Eve were removed from Eden. Their sons Cain and Abel offer a sacrifice to God, but God rejects Cain's offering. "So Cain was very angry, and his face fell. The Lord said to Cain, 'Why are you angry, and why has your face fallen? …you must rule over it.'"[2]

Cain got rejected, and was probably a little embarrassed too, so he got angry. God warned Cain that if he didn't properly manage his anger he was in serious danger. His anger pointed to something deep within him that needed to be dealt with. At that moment, Cain had a choice: Use his anger for good or evil.

The apostle Paul, who was repeating the words of King David, seemed to have no problem with anger in its right

THE GIFT OF ANGER **53**

place: "Be angry and do not sin; do not let the sun go down on your anger, and give no opportunity to the devil."[3]

Anger isn't a sin.

Jesus got angry. At one point he stormed through the courtyard of the temple in Jerusalem overturning tables. He was angry about how the religious leaders were abusing people. That was righteous anger. That's the kind of anger that's a force to confront injustice and defend the oppressed. You've probably felt anger at injustice. When you saw someone humiliated. Watched a child being emotionally or physically abused. Saw someone taking advantage of the poor. Seeing these things makes you want to take action. Like Jesus, we *should* get angry when we see injustice, and when it's within our power to do something, we should act. That is truly righteous anger. Righteous anger is real, but it's rare.

I've manhandled a few tables in my time, but I can't say it was because I was standing up for the weak. Hardly. It was because I had unmet expectations, blocked goals, or felt threatened. When I want something a certain way and it doesn't happen, I react. I get frustrated and annoyed. I respond with anger hoping to regain the balance of power. Can you relate?

Anger makes us feel powerful, which makes it appealing, especially if you feel like you're always being beaten down or abused. One counselor I know told me about a client who admitted that anger gave her the power she needed to survive. Losing that power frightened her. She told him, "I will never give up my anger. It motivates me and drives me to be a leader in life. If you live in forgiveness and grief, that is a lake, and people will drown you." Anger can drive you to the top, but it can also take you down in an instant.

Anger makes you *feel* powerful, but it actually causes you to lose control. Scientific studies have proven that your IQ drops when you're angry.[4] When we feel threatened we go primal. Fight or flight. Our body naturally responds to the threat with something called Diffuse Physiological Arousal (DPA). Brain function shifts from the pre-frontal cortex (our rational thinking area) to our cortex. Adrenaline kicks in. Our muscles tense. Our heart beats faster. Our pupils even dilate to help us hone in on the object threatening us. At that point, it's over. Reason and rational thinking are out the door. We may feel powerful, but we've lost control and we've actually lost IQ points. We've gotten dumber!

DPA also directly inhibits the part of the brain responsible for empathy, problem-solving, and strategic thinking.

It's impossible to creatively solve problems when you are angry because your brain isn't operating at full capacity.

ANGER AND YOUR BIGGEST REGRETS

God warned Cain, "…you must rule over [anger]." But Cain didn't. He lost control and ended up killing his brother. If you don't get your anger channeled and under control it will lead to disastrous results. It can also lead to missed opportunities and regret. I know this firsthand.

While I was working my way through college my boss started driving me crazy, so I applied for a transfer to another department. Requesting that transfer required approval from the boss I didn't like. There was no reason for her to deny my request, but she did. When I asked why, she said that my attendance record was questionable. I was furious. I had only missed one day of work in three years. I had been sick! Other people I worked with missed dozens of days of work for parties, hangovers, and family gatherings. She was just trying to harass me. I stormed out of her office.

Back in my office, I was fuming. I saw she was calling on the caller ID. I ignored the call. She just kept calling. Finally, I answered, "What!?" I yelled it. She demanded I come back and talk to her. I refused. We managed to avoid any interaction for the next few weeks. Shortly after that a position as a supervisor came open. I applied, but soon discovered I'd be interviewed by that same boss. The interview went well, but I didn't get the job. And I knew why. Anger made me feel powerful at the time, but ultimately it came back to haunt me.

I'm guessing you've got some of your own regrets when it comes to anger—the relationship that ended, the job you lost, whatever or whoever suffered—all because you let your anger mess things up.

So, let me throw down a challenge: It's time to take control of your anger and start using it for good. It's time to recognize there's a problem and get really honest about taking back true control. Being honest is the first key. Admit it's a problem. It's *your* problem. The problem isn't your kids, your spouse, your boss. It's you, and your anger.

Face it, you can't change the people in your life. But you can change you. Keep reading, because I'm going to show you how to start using anger as a force for good. But first, a quick chat with those people who think this chapter doesn't apply to them.

"BUT I DON'T GET ANGRY."

One of the most common responses I hear when I talk about anger is, "But I really don't get angry." It's hard for some people to acknowledge their anger. They call it frustration or being irritated. Some people are really good at suppressing anger or expressing it in a more socially acceptable manner. They don't explode or hit people or throw things, so they think they've got it under control. But that's often not the case.

I've found that those who believe they don't experience anger are usually those who have been hurt in the connection area. They fear anger because of the negative vibes it creates in relationships, so they suppress it. But anger is still there. It just looks different. How can you know if you're one of those people? Here are some more subtle expressions of anger.[5]

The Ticking Time Bomb—These folks have a long fuse. They rarely react at the moment of the incident. The anger builds slowly, sometimes over years, until one day the person explodes. Typically, these folks hold their anger in society and the explosion happens at home with family. Once they've exploded, they feel calm. It's all released and they feel great. They may even want to throw a party! "Hey, let's go out for pizza!" But everyone who was a victim of the explosion is hurt and cowering in fear—unsure if they can trust this sudden good will. They live in fear of when the next outburst will happen.

The Point Keeper—Point keepers also don't immediately react when they're offended or hurt. They file the hurt away, adding offense after offense to their inner list. When they finally get tipped over the edge, they unload, bringing up issues from years ago—the honeymoon incident, the time you forgot to pay the electric bill, the dumb thing you said at that party—things you may have never known even bothered them. They say they aren't angry, but holding a list of grievances that comes out when the victim least expects it? Like it or not, that's anger.

Captain Sarcastic—Yup. Sarcasm is a form of anger. It's just clever and quick. It feels safe. If you say something sarcastic and people respond negatively, you can always say, "Relax! Can't you take a joke?" But sarcasm is a form of anger disguised as humor.

The Velvet-Harpoon Champion—These folks are pleasant on the surface. They smile and put you at ease. But then they make a cutting remark in a deviously kind way. We've all met these folks. One lady came up to me after a four-week series of sermons I gave and said, "I loved this last message! It was the best of the four. You are finally teaching the Bible. Great job." She smiled and walked away. Apparently, she had some issues with the first few messages! These folks pretend to care, but lash out whenever they get a chance to do it in a "kind" way.

The Deep Freeze—When these people feel threatened, they become quiet and distant. Some won't speak to the person that hurt them for weeks, even if they live in the same home. Or apartment. Or dorm room. Silence is the weapon they use to force the other person to apologize, or to punish them for what they've done. They'll act like they are trying to take the high road and not lash out, but they *are* lashing out. They're just using silence and distance to do it rather than violence or yelling.

The Gang Fighter—Gang fighters only express anger when surrounded by friends. Being in a group gives them confidence to lash out. Exhibit A of this: a few married couples gets together and one spouse starts to make biting jokes to the group about their husband or wife. They use the safety they feel in a group as a chance to express grievances. A community around them gives them confidence in their anger.

The Guerrilla Fighter—Two words: Passive aggressive. These folks comply or agree with you to your face, but behind your back they gossip and undermine you. You rarely see their anger, but you sure feel the effects of it.

So odds are good, even if you say you don't get angry, that you do. It may just be in a subtler way. You can call it frustration or irritation or disappointment or whatever you want, but it's anger. And it's okay to admit you get angry. Really. We all deal with it. Remember, anger is just a response to your basic needs for safety, connection, or empowerment being threatened. The key is to make sure the anger doesn't limit you or hurt others.

So here's how you can start to use anger for good, rather than harm.

PAY ATTENTION

Pay attention to your negative feelings. Even little ones. Don't just ignore them or tell yourself this shouldn't be such a big deal. If you get irritated every time you are around a certain person, try to figure out why. Think about what emotions you feel when you're around that person. If something your wife does always sets you off, think about why. What is being threatened? If something bothers you, it's a big deal. When you feel annoyed or frustrated by something it's a sign, so don't waste it. Use it to evaluate what's happening deep inside you.

A female friend commented to me that she was annoyed about some pictures her friend was posting on Facebook, posing in a bikini. I asked what about the pictures made her so angry. She said she wasn't angry, just frustrated...But it was clearly bothering her.

*When you feel annoyed or frustrated by something it's a sign, so don't waste it. **Use** it.*

Everything in life is connected, so we started looking at what was happening around her that might be driving this frustration. Her husband was away on a business trip and she had just received some negative results from a doctor's report while he was gone. Stress was piling up. She got honest and admitted that she was worried her husband might see the pictures of their friend and it could cause him to fight a mental battle with lust. She was afraid of what this could do to their relationship. Her anger was driven by fear of damage to her and her husband's relationship, and maybe even by worrying that the health issue might make her less attractive to her husband.

This all played out in a simple Facebook post. Sure, my friend's anger was more subdued than outright rage, but that feeling within her was a sign of something deeper. Don't ignore anger or frustration. Pay attention.

Once you've started to pay attention to negative emotions and anger, here are three steps you can take to turn them into a force for good in your life.

1 — IDENTIFY WHAT CONSISTENTLY MAKES YOU ANGRY

Start tracking your anger. Make an anger journal. Take it with you in your pocket or purse. When you feel yourself getting angry (or even mildly frustrated) write down what happened, when it was, and who was involved. Here's an example:

Time:	7:45 am
Location:	on the road
People Involved:	other drivers
What Happened:	I'm going to be late because of traffic.

Traffic was the issue. Now, identify if it was about a threat to safety, connection, or control. For me, when it comes to traffic, it's not usually about my safety—we are driving slow as molasses. It isn't about my connection with others either—I have no desire to connect with other drivers in cars around me. Traffic is about my lack of control. I have no control over those drivers around me and they are controlling my schedule, making me late!

Here's another example:

Time:	*10:11 am*
Location:	*office*
People Involved:	*my boss and Gina*
What Happened:	*They met without me and didn't consider my ideas.*

What's the issue here? Well, it seems like a relational issue—a threat to your connection with others or self-esteem. Being left out doesn't feel good. It leaves you feeling invalidated. It makes you frustrated or even angry.

Keep track of your anger episodes for a week or two. While you read this book you'll probably find yourself remembering a few more instances from your past that made you really angry. Write those down too. Look for patterns.

CHECK OUT
WhyAmIAngry.info

It's a short quiz I created to help you identify what is really driving your anger. After you enter your responses you'll get a read-out that suggests what threat to your basic needs tends to get you riled up.

2 — WHEN YOU GET ANGRY, TAKE TIME OUT

The Apostle James offered a powerful formula for keeping your anger in check. He says: *Know this, my beloved brothers: let every person be quick to hear, slow to speak, slow to anger.*[6] Remember, when you feel yourself getting angry, your brain is kicking into fight-or-flight mode. It will rush to respond. But it isn't working at full, rational capacity. You may feel in control, but you aren't. You need to slow down. Love slows down. Anger speeds up.

To avoid doing or saying something you'll regret, step away from the situation. You may need to tell the person, "I can't talk about this right now. I need to calm down." If they push the issue, just get away. Take a walk. Go clean

Love slows down. Anger speeds up.

something (that works for me!). Go for a run. Exercise. For our safety and yours, please don't drive! You are prone to hurt someone. Do some physical activity to calm your body down and reset your brain.

Then, once you've calmed down, get your pre-frontal cortex firing again. Think it through. Use that brilliant mind of yours. Identify the threat that triggered your anger. Was it a threat to your safety and security? A threat to your connection with others or to your self-esteem? A threat to your empowerment or control? It's probably going to be the same thing every time. Don't just settle for knowing you're angry. Anyone can do that. Take the time to figure out *why*. You may need to say a prayer and ask God to show you which threat is creating your anger.

Don't. Skip. This. Step. You have to get this right for the next step to succeed.

When you identify exactly what is making you angry, you'll be more articulate in expressing what the issue really is, which will improve your chances of resolving the situation.

Once you've figured out the threat you are responding to, it's time to take the final step and express it. But because you took the time to get away, cool down, and think it through, you'll be able to express what you are truly feeling and do it without a bunch of emotional baggage.

3 — EXPRESS YOUR FEELINGS USING PRIMARY EMOTIONS

Anger is a secondary emotion. But to resolve things you need to use primary emotions. Address the primary issue. Just saying, "You made me angry!" won't get you anywhere. You need to express *why* you got angry, keeping in mind that anger is *your* issue. So keep it about that. Don't blame. It's too easy to sound like we're accusing someone of "making" us angry, or intentionally doing something to upset us, which usually isn't the case. Simply state, without accusing, how the situation made you feel. Use "I" statements, rather than "you" statements. I find this line to be helpful when expressing my feelings:

"When I found out _____, I felt_____."

Here are some examples:

"When I found out I had been left out of that meeting, I felt overlooked, like my ideas didn't matter."

"When I found out my shift was changed without telling me, I felt helpless."

"In our conversation, I felt belittled."

"When our money is spent in ways other than we've agreed on, I feel unsafe. I worry we won't have enough when we need it."

Sorting through primary emotions can be hard. It's a skill you get better and better at with time. Sometimes it's embarrassing to admit what was really bothering you. But to get the most out of your anger you need to do the work and think a little deeper. Here are some primary emotion words to help you describe what you felt:

- Threats to safety and security: I felt vulnerable, threatened, in danger, alone, ganged up on.

- Threats to connection and self-esteem: I felt like I was being compared, not good enough, belittled, invalidated.

- Threats to control and empowerment: I felt ignored, helpless, powerless, overwhelmed, weak, stupid.

Assume the best about people. Sure, there are some people who are just intentionally mean, but generally people aren't trying to make you angry. In fact, more often than not they'll have no idea what they did or said that triggered your anger. That's because it's not about them or what they do. It's about you and how you felt.

When you express your anger using primary emotions, and you keep the message about you and your reaction, people can relate to you. It gives them something to work with. It also gives you greater insight into who you are—your motivations, drives, and fears. With that knowledge, you can begin a journey of self-exploration that'll help you live better, love better, and walk in the freedom that God has for you.

Can you imagine what a difference it could make if you started to see anger for the gift it is? Instead of letting anger turn you into an out-of-control, rage-aholic, what if you learned to channel it—to use it for good. You could become nearly invincible! Every annoyance or frustration would become a chance to get more in touch with the unseen forces that are driving you. Rather than offense and rage, anger could become your greatest ally in gaining insight into what's keeping you from being your true self. Anger could help you grow. Every time you felt anger it could turn into a chance to become stronger and more insightful.

You have the capacity to control your anger and use it to help yourself become all God intends for you to be. Anger is a gift. Don't fear it. Don't ignore it. Use it!

CHAPTER 4

INTERPRETATIONS AND YOUR FAMILY (OR HOW YOU GOT THIS WAY)

The single biggest problem in communication is the illusion that it has taken place. —GEORGE BERNARD SHAW

Men are disturbed not by things but by the view they take of them. —EPICTETUS

To this day I'm still not sure what I told that

Chinese cab driver, but it nearly caused a disaster.

Our team had been around Beijing for several weeks, and now we were taking another train to visit a small town in Western China. I sent the team ahead with all of our bags and I was going to pick up some authentic regional food,

Kan Da Ji, (aka Kentucky Fried Chicken) for the train ride. I grabbed my Chinese phrasebook and told a cab driver to take my team to the train station. They sped away. Then I flagged a cab and headed to pick up the food.

I got to the train station about forty minutes later, expecting them to be waiting at the entrance. They were nowhere to be found. And they had no phone. We were twenty minutes from boarding when I finally got a call from them. They weren't sure where the cab driver had taken them, but it was clearly not the train station. We managed to do a three-way call with a friend of the cab driver who spoke English and about fifteen minutes later, just before the train boarded, they got to the station and we all rushed on board.

When people ask me if I speak Chinese I always think back to this debacle and say, "Just enough to cause major problems."

Mandarin Chinese gets complicated. It's made up of single syllables. *Ma, da, bei, fung, la,* etc. Every syllable has four potential tones. The tones are simply called first, second, third, and fourth tones. These tones, or contours, are represented in Latin letters (the letters we use) by specific accent marks. If you don't get the tone right you can end up saying something completely different than what you intend. For example, depending on the tone, the simple word "ma" can mean *mother*, or *to bother*, or *horse*, or *to scold*. To add more complexity, "ma" can also be used at the end of a sentence to indicate a question was just asked. In the hands of an unskilled linguist (like me) Mandarin can get confusing. It's easy to communicate the completely wrong thing.

Know what's even more complex and nuanced than Mandarin Chinese?

People.

No two are exactly alike. Our personalities and experiences combine to create an infinite number of possible responses to any single situation. Depending on personality and past history two people can have the same experience and interpret it in completely different ways. An experience can create a hurt in the area of safety for one person while creating hurt in the area of connection or abandonment for another. A situation that deeply wounds one person may barely be noticed by another. Even with the very same experience, different people can process it differently. It's not what happens to you that has the impact, it's how you interpret what happens.

When I was in the sixth grade, my parents were church planters. Translation: we were poor. For a few years our family qualified for government-subsidized school lunch due to our financial situation. This was terribly embarrassing for me. I would always wait until everyone else had gone through the lunch line to grab my tray. I didn't want

*It's not what happens to you that has the impact, it's how you **interpret** what happens.*

people to know that I got lunch for forty cents just by telling the cashier my name.

I was talking with my sister recently about how ashamed I was about that discounted lunch. She commented that it bothered her that she had to pay a different price. She saw others got it free and it seemed unfair. She wasn't embarrassed. In fact, it seemed like injustice to her. Same experience, very different response.

PATTERNS OF INTERPRETATION

We figure out early in life what brings pain and what brings comfort. We develop a consistent series of response patterns to help minimize pain and maximize comfort. If we've learned that humor works to deflect criticism from our peers, we adopt it into our personality. If ingesting smoke, alcohol, or drugs gives us a calm or invincible feeling, we keep doing it. If throwing a fit keeps authority-types off our back, we'll keep throwing fits. If ignoring people who intimidate us works, we use that. We figure out what patterns get us what we want and, without realizing it, those patterns become habit.

In his book, *The Power of Habit,* Charles Duhigg says "Habits...emerge because the brain is constantly looking for ways to save effort...When a habit emerges, the brain stops fully participating in decision making. It stops working so hard, or diverts focus to other tasks. So unless you deliberately fight a habit—unless you find new routines—the pattern will unfold automatically."[1]

Your mind never shuts off. It's constantly working, receiving and storing new information. Because it's always working it wants some consistency and predictability so it can take a break. Habits are what your mind uses to create some predictability in this constantly changing world. They save our brain energy. Habits eventually become second nature. A Duke University study that found more than forty percent of the actions we perform each day aren't actual decisions, but habits.[2]

When habits of thought and action are based on shame-based beliefs we end up consistently operating in a dysfunctional way.

Even though you may not be thinking about it, your brain is constantly using data it has collected to interpret the world around you. We are always interpreting. Erwin McManus explains it this way:

> *"We are interpreters. This is the way we are designed. We are translators of meaning, and thus everything we see, hear, smell, touch, taste, and experience is processed through all our previous experiences and perceptions. We don't see people for who they are; we see them through the filter of everyone we've ever known. We don't see circumstances as they are; we see them through the filter of everything we've ever experienced. No experience is an experience in isolation."[3]*

Our defense mechanisms of self-absorption, self-gratification, and control are habit-based. Our mind, like a super computer with unlimited storage, remembers everything. If it feels threatened with shame, it responds with a defense mechanism.

YOUR UNIQUE TAKE

You've probably been in a conversation where you started getting angry, but you didn't know why. In that moment, your brain interpreted that something about this conversation was similar to a conversation you've had before, and the last time you were in a conversation like this it didn't go well. Your brain starts ringing warning bells and you go into protection mode, using your habit-based responses, without even knowing exactly what is bothering you. Your brain read a stimulus, interpreted it one way or another, and *boom*! It responded.

When habits of thought and action are based on shame-based beliefs we end up consistently operating in a dysfunctional way.

The problem is we can misinterpret situations. It's like having the wrong prescription glasses. We may not see things accurately. If our lenses are distorted by bad past experiences we can easily misread the most harmless of situations.

- *The last time a guy talked to me about my work/life balance, he dumped me. This guy is talking about it now. Oh no! He's going to dump me. I'd better dump him first.*

- *The last time I addressed bad behavior in my employees, they quit. If I address this bad behavior everyone will leave. I'll be alone with more work. I'll just ignore it.*

Things really get off-track when we start to form beliefs about how the world works from those wrong interpretations.

- *Relationships always end in pain.*

- *All men (or women) will eventually leave and hurt me.*

- *Everything I touch ends up falling to pieces.*

- *Confrontation makes people leave me.*

- *People aren't there for you when you really need them.*

One particular client I worked with believed that everyone was out to take advantage of her. She was so persuasive that I went to bat for her in a situation where she was certain she was being abused. But as more details emerged, from objective viewpoints, I realized that her reality was distorted. She was seeing hurt in normal, everyday challenges we all face. But to her, these were unique attacks aimed at her. Past hurt made her believe that everyone was out to get her.

We are all prone to develop wrong beliefs based on past experiences. No matter how real or true a situation may seem to us, it's quite possible that our worldview has been tainted by past experiences. We have to be open to the possibility that we might not be seeing things as they really are

FAMILY ISSUES

In her book, *Crossing the Tracks for Love,* Ruby K. Payne talks about the unspoken rules of social classes. Different socio-economic classes have different views on things as diverse as food, relationships, education, and, of course, money. These views are caught, not taught. You pick them up by observing the world where you grow up.

These rules of class impact everything. For example, in poverty the most important factor in a meal is quantity. *Did you get enough?* But the extremely wealthy value presentation of the food. *Was the presentation pleasing?* (Which is why, when you go to an expensive restaurant, your meal comes on a huge white plate with a tiny piece of meat, one sliver of vegetable, and some parsley. Beautiful! But I'm still hungry.) In the middle class the issue is, *How did the food taste?* These little nuances are assimilated into the way we view the world without us ever realizing it.

Typically, through education or marriage, you'll either move up or down one class within your lifetime. But unless you're taught otherwise, you'll still operate by the unspoken rules you learned growing up. If you grew up in poverty, watching your parents live from paycheck to paycheck, but as an adult you get a great job that earns you a healthy paycheck, you may now be a member of the middle class. But if you haven't learned how money works and the disciplines of investing, it's quite possible that you will continue living from paycheck to paycheck, just with larger amounts of money.

Often times folks who shift from one socioeconomic status to another feel out of place and awkward in their new world. They have the money and status, but still feel uncomfortable because they don't understand that those around them actually see life through a completely different lens.

Just like those unspoken worldviews of social class, we all carry around beliefs that we caught from our family about ourselves and others. We learned most of these rules before we were able to rationally think them through. As kids, we didn't know any better. We just trusted that the adults around us had life figured out. If Uncle Joe said our family has always been oppressed and poor, we believed it. If grandpa said that people can't be trusted and everyone lies, we believed it. If mom said all men are violent and angry, we believed it. If a teacher said we weren't creative or smart, we believed it.

Most of our strongest beliefs weren't taught, they were caught. We observed and, in the absence of any evidence to conflict with what we saw, we came to our own conclusions based on the limits of our personal experience.

We had nothing to compare those beliefs to, so we accepted them as being how the world works. If Dad hit Mom when he was mad, this seemed normal. If Mom covered for Dad when he was drunk and missed work, this seemed normal. If subtle emotional manipulation was how our family got us to behave, we learned this as a normal way of dealing with others. If we never talked about emotions in our family, this was normal. These became the pattern for how we believe the world works, even if they aren't healthy or accurate perceptions. Today, if you haven't taken the time to recognize them, those shame-based beliefs and patterns are still impacting you. But once you acknowledge them, you can do something about it.

BREAKING THE CYCLE

For better or worse, our parents pass down to us what they got from their parents. If we don't ever question what they modeled, we'll pass down the same to our kids. Issues that aren't dealt with are always passed down. That's why so many people often repeat the same mistakes as their parents, even though they swore they wouldn't. We all live out the beliefs and habits we've developed. We can try all we want to make different choices, but we all act based on what we believe. If you've got beliefs that are dysfunctional, you'll end up with results in your life that are too. If you want to break a shame-based cycle you've got to identify wrong beliefs in your family and replace them with a new belief system. A system based in truth.

Issues that aren't dealt with are always passed down.

Acknowledging where our parents got it wrong can seem disloyal, or just plain ungrateful. It can be hard to admit that our parents made mistakes. The goal here isn't to get all riled up about how your parents messed you up. The goal is to identify what wrong shame-based beliefs and mindsets we may have inadvertently adopted that are now limiting us. As you uncover those beliefs, you'll usually find that they developed in response to some challenges or hurts in your parents' lives. If you've been upset with your parents, feeling like they gave you a bad start in life, acknowledging *their* past can help you see that they were doing the best they could, trying to manage what life handed them.

My grandfather had polio as a child and lost his ability to walk. He was given a free surgery in a hospital far from his home in southern Louisiana to restore his mobility. His parents took him to the hospital, but because they were poor, they couldn't afford to stick around. So they went home. My grandfather, still a young child, stayed in that hospital undergoing surgery, all alone for weeks. I know he felt helpless and afraid. He probably felt abandoned too. That surgery changed his life and he went on to be very financially successful. He did a great job caring for his family and he was extremely generous with his grandkids. But for most of his life he was in a perpetual state of anxiety, worried about his own safety. Because he was physically disabled, he often resorted to subtle emotional manipulation to get what he wanted. My grandma was also disabled, so she had similar defenses.

My mom grew up under this tension. There was an undercurrent of fear and guilt in her home. No one directly confronted anything. It was all hush-hush and subtle. My mom picked up this anxiety, believing she needed to be hyper-vigilant, always on the lookout for danger. When I was in elementary school, she went through a difficult few years of oppressive anxiety. I felt that stress. But I didn't understand it. I remember wondering if my mother was going to die. It was a lot for a kid to shoulder. At that moment, some of that anxiety got passed on to me.

Fortunately, my mom decided to break the cycles of guilt, anxiety, and shame in my family. She decided she wasn't going to pass that on to us. She took the courageous step to get counseling. She prayed a lot. But the biggest step she took was when she and my father obeyed God and moved our family to the war-torn country of Guatemala to be missionaries. Definitely not the best place for someone riddled with anxiety. But that courageous decision was a major leap forward in our family. Mom conquered her fear by obedience to God and set a new standard.

You can do the same.

Your decisions to be courageous, adopt new mindsets, and set a new standard in your family will be a model to those around you. Your family may not understand it right off the bat. They might even get angry and accuse you of thinking you are better than them. They'll remind you of all the shame in your family. They'll tell you where you came from and how you're rejecting your history. They'll tell you to know your place. Don't believe them! Don't let them bring you down. Be kind, but prove them wrong by setting a new standard in your family. Be the one who takes your family to a new level.

Mom broke a cycle of anxiety and guilt in our family and replaced it with courage and confidence. She changed her beliefs and she changed our family's future. And I'm forever grateful for that! Sure, she didn't always get it right. No parent does. There were times, particularly when she was dealing with major anxiety, that she didn't know how to confront my strong personality. She'd fall back on what she learned from her father and mother – emotional manipulation. But mom realized that she didn't have to live that way anymore. She started living out of who she truly was in Christ. And we all benefitted from her being who she really is.

The same will happen when you make the decision for your family.

DIGGING UP THE FAMILY SKELETONS

I love the story of King Josiah. He became King of Judah at the tender age of eight. Josiah came from one messed-up family. His grandfather Manasseh was known for being one of the most ungodly men to ever rule Judah. The writers of the Bible didn't pull any punches describing his grandfather's failures. "Manasseh led them astray to do more evil than the nations had done whom the Lord destroyed before the people of Israel."[4] Not a good way to be remembered. The deck seemed stacked against Josiah from the beginning.

By the time Josiah came to the throne, his family had led their country into turmoil. Judah had completely forgotten God and they were worshipping idols in the temple of Yahweh. But in his teens, Josiah decided it was time to break the cycle. He went on a rampage, destroying idols all over the country. He destroyed altars that his own grandfather had set up. He reestablished worship of Yahweh as the one true God.

But Josiah wasn't finished. He went on to do something that seems borderline maniacal. "Then Josiah turned around and noticed several tombs in the side of the hill. He ordered that the bones be brought out, and he burned them on the altar at Bethel to desecrate it."[5] Did you catch that? Josiah dug up dead people and burned their bones. *Geez!* That was someone's grandpa he dug up!

Why did he get so aggressive? Well, when you read further you see that those were the bones of the pagan prophets who had done so much damage to Israel. I can't help but wonder if Josiah was so intense in his response because he wanted to symbolically uproot the harm his parents had passed down. He was saying, "The dysfunction stops here!"

For all you folks who take things literally, let me make this clear: Don't go digging up your local cemetery! But I do think you should consider doing some symbolic digging. Start to explore your family history. Start to explore your family's mindsets. What do the people who raised you believe about how life works? What do they believe about relationships, money, work, and God?

Like an archeologist, do some careful excavating. Deal with the past gently and cautiously. Interview that aunt who seems to have all the dirt on the family secrets nobody wants to talk about. Humbly begin to ask your family about their story. Put yourself in the shoes of those who impacted you. Once you know more of their story, try to imagine what it would have been like growing up like they did. Find out what struggles your parents and grandparents faced.

Ask things like:

- What difficult historical events did my family members live through?

- Were they involved in any global conflicts? Wars?

- Did my grandparents grow up during the Great Depression?

- Did any of my family members suffer from illness or chronic pain?

- Were my family members immigrants? If so, what kind of environment did they leave in their home country? War, gang violence, economic ruin?

- What corner of the hurt triangle do I think my parents struggle with? Abandonment, rejection, humiliation?

Never underestimate how events like these may have shaped your own history.

Remember, it isn't disloyal to admit that your family made mistakes. We've all got issues. But that doesn't mean past problems and mindsets need to impact us for the rest of our lives. When we identify what is affecting us, we can change it.

The best part about this process is it will help you develop compassion and understanding for the challenges your family members faced. You'll see why they developed their defense mechanisms to cover shame. But most importantly, you'll start

When we identify what is affecting us, we can change it.

to see that those defenses and mindsets that got passed down don't have to define you. I'm absolutely certain that if you'll embrace and acknowledge all of your history—good, bad, and ugly—God will redeem it. He'll actually turn it into something that makes the world a better place.

DIVINE INTERVENTION

Joseph, the son of Jacob, came from an uber-dysfunctional family. There was favoritism, deception, and manipulation. If that wasn't enough, his own brothers threw him into a pit, sold him into slavery, then lied to their father about what they had done.

Joseph's family completely messed up his life. He was taken to another country and sold like some kind of animal. Then things got worse. His character was maligned, he was lied about, and he spent years in prison for a crime he didn't commit. Joseph's family seemed to have destroyed his future.

Until God stepped in.

Through a divine revelation, Joseph was promoted, overnight, to be the second most powerful man in Egypt. A few years later his brothers came looking for help and supplies during a drought. Joseph saw the big picture of what God had been doing. He told his brothers, "You meant evil against me, but God meant it for good, to bring it about that many people should be kept alive, as they are today."[6]

God wants to do the same thing for you and your family history. He wants to give you your own divine revelation that propels you into becoming all he has for you. Your family history may have held you back up to this point, but if you'll get honest and identify where things went wrong, he can redeem even the worst things that happened to you. And you'll pass that new legacy of redemption down to your family.

MAKE THE DECISION

Now, imagine what could happen if you decided to really do this. To say, "I'm stopping the family line of dysfunction here. It ends now." Imagine if you identified the dysfunction and bad mindsets your family has lived with for years—emotional manipulation, greed, anger, anxiety, depression—recognize its limiting power in your life, and then eliminate that power by embracing what this book is about: true freedom in Christ. Think about the difference it would make in the lives of your kids. Your grandkids. Think about the message it could speak to the rest of your family. Think about the peace it would bring you to know that you aren't going to repeat the same mistakes and embrace the wrong mindsets that limited you.

It's a new day. And you are a new person in Christ. You are who *he* says you are.

Now, I know you are all pumped up and ready to change the future of your family. But don't skip the work of exploration. Set aside some time to explore your family history. Start gently asking some questions. Don't ignore your heritage. Write out what your family believes about time and work and money and relationships and God. Try to understand what happened in their lives that made them believe those things. Then line those beliefs you inherited or adopted up against what God says is true. If you've been living with a wrong belief system, now is the time to change it!

And that change starts now. We are about to dive into the game plan for making a lasting change in your life.

CHAPTER 5

THE ART OF WAR

A true Christian is one who has not only peace of conscience, but war within. He may be known by his warfare as well as by his peace. —J.C. RYLE, ANGLICAN BISHOP

The Chinese game of Wei Qi (pronounced WAY-Chee) has been around for over 2,500 years. The Japanese call the game *Go*. Everywhere I went in China I saw people playing this game. Two players each start with one-hundred and eighty "stones," on a nineteen-by nineteen-grid. One player gets black stones, the other gets white. At first glance it looks like chess, but victory in Wei Qi is about winning through indirect confrontation. Unlike chess, where you attack and remove the pieces of your opponent, Wei

Qi takes a much more nuanced approach. You win by encircling your opponent at various places around the board. Wei Qi actually means *encircling game.*

The game is such a huge part of Chinese culture that David Lai, a professor at Army War College in Pennsylvania, is convinced that if you really want understand Chinese global political strategy, the key is to look at the game of Wei Qi. Chinese leaders historically choose the long game of encircling their opponents without direct confrontation. Lai's theory was so compelling that even the great diplomat Henry Kissinger adopted this framework for understanding Chinese strategy in world politics.[1]

The way you win in Wei Qi sounds a whole lot like the strategies of a Chinese general named Sun Tzu, who authored a little book called *The Art of War.* This book is filled with all sorts of esoteric, Zen-type statements like:

> *"If you know the enemy and you know yourself, you need not fear the result of a hundred battles."*

> *"The supreme art of war is to subdue the enemy without fighting."*

Sun Tzu says wars are won by fighting the battle on a higher level. "Victorious warriors win first and then go to war, while defeated warriors go to war first and then seek to win." Honestly, the book feels a little too passive for me. I prefer direct confrontation. Let's not think too long or skirt around the issue. Face off with it. I like to believe I can conquer and overpower anything I confront. I tend to approach making changes in my life with that same strategy of direct confrontation.

The problem is, no matter how hard I try there are still areas in my life I just can't seem to beat. I muster every ounce of willpower, but I still struggle with anger. I get insecure. I try to be someone I'm not. I fall back into my old habits. You're human, so I know you can relate. You've probably begun to wonder if change is actually possible.

In what's probably one of the most relatable passages in the entire Bible, the Apostle Paul talks about this frustration we all face: "I do not understand my own actions. For I do not do what I want, but I do the very thing I hate...I have the desire to do what is right, but not the ability to carry it out..."[2]

We've all been there. It gets discouraging. How many self-help books have we read that helped for a few days or weeks, but we ultimately gave up on? How many conferences and sermons have we sat through and decided we're really gonna do it this time—we are going to change. But we don't. At least not to the level we really want.

Let me lead with some good news. People *can* change, but I think the reason most people don't is because we've been going about it all wrong. We've been working from a Western, full-frontal confrontation model. But I believe real, lasting change comes from something closer to Sun Tzu's tactics.

THE DYNAMICS OF CHANGE

In orientation for my master's degree in counseling, a soft-spoken professor sat the entire group of us new students in a circle. He asked why we wanted to join the program. We had lots of different reasons. The professor affirmed our reasons, but then got a little somber and said, "Don't get your hopes up too high on how much of a difference you can make. People don't really change. You'll only see real change in three to five percent of the people you work with."

At the time I wasn't a very optimistic person (I've gotten better), but the statement still didn't sit well with me. Is it really that bad? We all change some, right? I mean, I like to think I've changed a little. But the more I learned about change the more I came to see why he made that statement. The statistics aren't promising. True, lasting change in people is actually quite rare. We've all been disappointed when someone we love promised to change, took a few steps forward, but then reverted back to their old ways. We've also been disappointed with ourselves when we can't change. It's hard to be optimistic about our ability to change when we look at reality.

But while I was studying for that degree I witnessed something firsthand that convinced me that gentle old professor was wrong. People can change. While in school I worked as an associate pastor. In the church where I served there was a guy named Chuck who, in all honesty, I really wanted to kick out of the church. (Yes, I was basically a horrible pastor, but hear me out.)

When Chuck wasn't standing out front smoking and complaining about the weather to people entering the church, he was cornering people in the foyer whining about everything—including the church. He never went into the service. He just stood around the foyer looking for people to complain to. At one staff meeting I actually brought up asking him to leave the church, but it didn't fly. So I had to instruct the greeters at the front to keep him out of the foyer. But somehow, he always managed to sneak back in and irritate everyone.

I figured I'd just have to live with Chuck. Paul the Apostle had a thorn in his flesh,[3] and now, alas, so did I. But something mind-blowing happened. Chuck found out he had a terminal illness. To cope, he started meeting with a counselor at our church named Catherine.

At that same time, I was gone two Sundays in a row. When I returned I almost couldn't recognize Chuck. He seemed taller, his face was glowing, and the dude actually smiled at me! I kept hearing that he was going around apologizing to people he had hurt or offended. People who had avoided him like the plague now hung out with him and enjoyed it. Completely flabbergasted by what I was seeing, I went to Catherine. "What the heck happened to him?"

Cat smiled and said something to the effect of, "He got courageous and decided to change. He faced his past and forgave."

Chuck died a few months later. Loads of people showed up at his funeral. Lots of them were people who just a few months earlier despised the guy. They told glowing stories about how much his apology meant to them and what a powerful change they had seen in him. He had become an inspiration to hundreds of people in our church.

Sure, stats say it's nearly impossible to change, but God says otherwise.

THE PRICE OF CHANGE

Change is hard. Positive, lasting change doesn't just happen. It takes intentionality and focus. It takes insight, because it starts in a place we can't see. As Richard Foster says, "The needed change within us is God's work, not ours. The demand is for an inside job, and only God can work from the inside."[4]

You can change your environment—move to a new town, get a new job, get a makeover, or make more money—but that will never solve the real issues holding you back. Because we aren't fighting against flesh and blood or what we see.[5]

Jesus' main complaint with the Pharisees was that they were hung up on externals. "Don't you see that nothing that enters a person from the outside can defile them? For it doesn't go into their heart…What comes out of a person is what defiles them." Jesus goes through a laundry list of sins, then says, "All these evils come from inside…"[6] Jesus made it crystal clear that our real problem is hidden deep in our hearts.

You'll never beat the power of shame and your false self through direct confrontation or will power. No amount of behavior modification or counseling will bring lasting change. You may be able to change a few habits here and there, but beating the deeply engrained patterns and wrong beliefs will only happen with a different kind of approach.

"WE'LL MAKE THEM CHANGE!"

I'm gonna take a quick detour for a history and philosophy lesson.

When Mao Zedong marched into Beijing in January of 1949 he was leading a massive military force known as the People's Liberation Army. Mao ran off the old regime of Chiang Kai-Shek who fled with 600,000 of his supporters to an island called Formosa, or Taiwan. Back on the mainland Mao took over China and created a communist government.

You'll never beat the power of shame and your false self through direct confrontation or will power.

Shortly after the revolution, Mao stared persecuting Christians and a number of other religions. Pure communist ideology is founded on atheism. Karl Marx said that religion was like a drug for people, keeping them detached from reality.[7] Pure philosophical communism and Christianity are deeply at odds because communism is built on a philosophy called *dialectical materialism.* This philosophy says that nothing exists except physical matter and its movements and modifications. Basically, something is only real if you can see it, taste it, touch it, etc. Materialist philosophy teaches that all beliefs and philosophies are a direct result of what can be physically perceived. So if you want to change someone's beliefs or behaviors, you change their environment—what can be seen.

Christianity says the complete opposite. Christians believe that there is a very real, unseen spirit world that impacts the physical material world. Jesus taught that you can change no matter how bad the environment may be, because change starts on the inside. But if you don't believe in a spiritual reality, you'll resort to changing things from the outside in.

And there are plenty of people who buy into that idea. After all, it's easier. You can see external changes, so it feels like you're getting immediate results. But when you try to change the unseen world of thoughts, emotions, and desires by changing the material world history has shown it will always bring disastrous results, no matter how sincere you may be.

The most conservative estimates say that over 30 million (yes, *million!*) Chinese died during Mao's revolution. To put that in perspective, that's ten percent of the current population of the United States. The crazy part is, these deaths didn't happen in the revolution to overthrow the previous leaders of China. Nope, these were the direct result of reforms implemented by Mao himself—the guy who was supposed to be liberating China!

Compare the Chinese revolution to another revolution that began two thousand years earlier. Israel was looking for a savior to free them from Roman oppression. Jesus came on the scene and worked his way through the countryside of Israel, drawing huge crowds and teaching about a new Kingdom. He backed it all up with the power to heal and cast out demons. That got peoples' attention.

People became more and more convinced that it was just a matter of time before Jesus was going to free them from the Romans. But the army Jesus built never started arming themselves. In fact, when his disciple Peter did start swinging a sword, Jesus rebuked him: "Put away your sword…those who use the sword will die by the sword."[8]

When Jesus rode into Jerusalem on Palm Sunday, he received a king's welcome. But the whole scene was slightly askew. Rather than ride a white stallion, this king showed up on a donkey. But the crowd still waved palm branches, welcoming the man they were certain was going to liberate them from their oppressors.

But within a few days that crowd flip-flopped. Jesus seemed out of his mind to them. Instead of attacking the Romans, Jesus attacked the religious system of his own people. They were so disillusioned that within a few short days they begged their oppressors to crucify him.

Jesus had a different game plan. Rather than millions dying in a bloody war or through aggressive social reforms, Jesus led a different kind of revolution. A revolution where only one man died. And through the power of his death, we got freedom from sin and shame. Jesus forgives. He re-stores. He redeems. He gives us a new identity.

Our job is to walk in that new identity, our true self in Christ. Strangely enough, even though it's all a work of God's Spirit within us, we have a part to play in becoming who we are in Christ. Because lasting transformation only happens when we partner with God and give him free reign in our lives.

ENTERING THE UNSEEN WORLD

Every Sunday while we were in Beijing we attended a church called Beijing International Christian Fellowship (BICF). The Chinese government only allows foreigners to attend this English-speaking church. If you go there, you have to show your passport to get in. People from dozens of countries show up there for worship in English.

Lasting transformation only happens when we partner with God and give him free reign in our lives.

It was while we attended BICF that I was first introduced to a book called *The Celebration of Discipline* by Richard Foster. The timing couldn't have been more perfect. Foster's book went hand-in-glove with what I was learning about the false self and how to become who God says you truly are.

Richard Foster started his book with these words: "Superficiality is the curse of our age...The desperate need today is not for a greater number of intelligent people, or gifted people, but for deep people."[9] Our whole world is focused on outside appearances. We love things to *look* good. There are dozens of TV shows about transformations and total makeovers. There's something appealing about seeing something shabby transformed into something esthetically pleasing.

I heard a host of one of these shows say, "Once you feel better about how you look on the outside, you'll feel better about yourself on the inside." *Hmm.* That's a nice thought, but every day I talk to people who look great on the outside—they're beautiful and intelligent, some are at the top of their field—but once you get to know them, you see they're as insecure, depressed, and overwhelmed as the rest of us.

Working on fixing what we see will only bring superficial change. We need a solution that starts somewhere deeper than what we see.

YOUR THREE PARTS

Genesis 1:27 says we were created in God's image. That's a complex truth. It has dimensions that go far beyond our limited knowledge. But there is one element of that truth that helps bring some major insight on how lasting change happens. God is three-in-one. And so are we. The Apostle Paul talks about these three parts when he prays, "Now may the God of peace himself sanctify you completely, and may your whole spirit and soul and body be kept blameless at the coming of our Lord Jesus Christ."[10]

We are a spirit, soul, and body all in one. The easiest way to grasp what this looks like is to think of it in terms of a target with three rings.

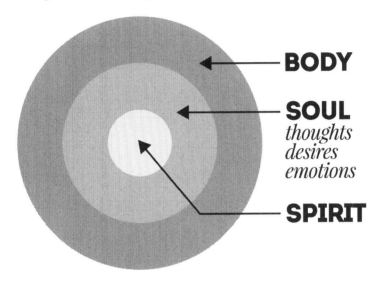

BODY

SOUL
thoughts
desires
emotions

SPIRIT

The outer ring is the body, or flesh. It's what we see. We dress it up, exercise it, feed it, and do our best to present a good image to the world. It's what we use to gather information about the world through our senses of touch, taste, hearing, seeing, and smell.

Just inside that outer ring of the body is the soul. This is the first unseen element of who we are. The Greek word

Paul uses for soul is *psuche.* We get our English word *psyche,* directly from this word. Psychology is the study of the soul.

Watchman Nee, a great Christian leader and martyr, who died at the hands of the Chinese communist government, broke the soul down into three parts: thoughts, desires, and emotions.[11] We can't see thoughts or desires or emotions, but we see the results. We make decisions based on our thoughts and desires. We act out on emotions. Much of what we do in our bodies is directly connected to what is going on in our *psuche*, or soul.

But the soul isn't where it ends. There is an even deeper part of us. At the center of those circles, the bull's-eye, is the spirit. This is where lasting change starts. As Paul Tournier says, "True inner healing…is not to be found on the level of psychology, but only in the realm of the spirit."[12]

Before we received Christ's gift of salvation we were "dead in our trespasses." But when we received Christ's gift, Christ "made us alive together with Christ"[13] At that moment, we are justified by his grace.[14] When he sees me (and you), it's Just as If I'd never sinned. We ask for forgiveness. God gives it. It's a done deal. You and God are all good in that moment. You are God's child. Perfect. Sinless. That's your new identity. That's your true self.

John says it this way: "Dear friends, we are already God's children, but he has not yet shown us what we will be like when Christ appears."[15]

Your sins are forgiven, your spirit is alive in Christ, but that's only the beginning. From there we start a lifelong process of bringing our emotions, desires, thoughts, and actions in line with the Spirit of God within us. As Ed Welch explains it, "When you are touched, you are changed. Zap. It happens in a moment. But it can take some of us quite a while to catch up with what Jesus did."[16] We're all new in Christ. The fullness of his power is within us. And now it's time to start embracing that reality. We have to get rid of our old, limiting mindsets based in shame and embrace the power of who we really are inside, through Christ.

TAKE ME BACK TO WHAT I KNOW

God used some pretty mind-blowing displays of power to free the children of Israel from oppression and slavery in Egypt. They marched out with baskets full of loot and their heads held high. But within just a few short days of this amazing deliverance, the children of Israel were begging to go back to Egypt, where they were slaves.[15] They longed for what was familiar, even though it was slavery. We are all prone to do the same. We forget how bad things used to be. One woman said it this way, "I know my life was a mess back there. But at least I knew the names of all the streets."

The children of Israel were out of Egypt, but it took forty years in the desert to get Egypt out of them. We are all in the same process of getting our old ways out of us.

In *The Screwtape Letters*, C.S. Lewis tells a fictional story of a demon whose job is to keep humans in bondage to Satan's power. In one particular letter, the head mentor-demon is concerned that his apprentice allowed his "patient" to become a Christian. But he comments, "There is no need to despair; hundreds of these adult converts have been reclaimed after a brief sojourn in the enemy's camp and are now with us. All the *habits* of the patient, both mental and bodily, are still in our favor."[18]

> *The children of Israel were out of Egypt, but it took forty years in the desert to get Egypt out of them.*

Shame and sin may have lost say over our eternal destiny, but if we aren't intentional about embracing our new identity, we'll slip back into the bondage of our false self. It's way too easy to go back to what's familiar.

Hanging out with Jesus gave Peter a new identity and destiny. He went from being a rough fisherman to a fisher of men. But when they came to arrest Jesus, Peter flipped out and slipped back into his old, familiar ways. He pulled out a sword and started swinging. We learn a lot about what's deep inside us when we get stressed. It's easier to act like a Christian than to react like one. Those reactions reveal whether we're living from the true or the false self.

The story is told of a famous marble sculptor who was asked how he made such life-like figures. He said, "I simply chip away everything that doesn't look like the sculpture I'm creating." Deep inside us is the fullness of God's Spirit. It's already there. We already have his image imprinted on us. Job number one in the Christian life is to allow God to chip away our defenses of self-absorption, self-gratification, and control and trade them in for love, joy, peace, patience, kindness, goodness, gentleness, and self-control.[19] That's what Paul is talking about when says, "Work out your own salvation with fear and trembling, for it is God who works in you, both to will and to work for his good pleasure."[20] We are new in Christ. Now we have to become who we already are.

That means we have to get our thoughts, desires, and emotions in line with who God says we are now. It's a total renovation. C.S. Lewis compares this process to inviting Jesus to fix up your house, but after he has fixed the leaks and plumbing he starts knocking out walls and adding entire new additions. The process is uncomfortable and we start asking, "What on earth is He up to? The explanation is that He is building quite a different house from the one you thought of...You thought you were being made into a decent little cottage: but He is building a palace. He intends to come and live in it Himself."[21]

> *We are new in Christ. Now we have to become who we already are.*

Here's the paradox of this whole renovation: It's all God's work, but we have a part to play. Our part comes through discipline. Specifically, spiritual discipline.

When you want to get strong physically, you get disciplined and start working out and watching what you eat. When you want to get strong spiritually, it's the same process. It's a slow process of stretching and pushing yourself and being intentional about what goes into your soul. But if you are committed you'll see change.

A SLOW BUILD

My wife Emily and I lived in Peru for a few years. When we first got there I was constantly sick. We lived at 11,000 feet of altitude. It's hard on your body. One day I decided I'd had enough. I got serious about working out and eating right. A friend and I started going to the gym every day. There were days I didn't want to go because I was tired. But my friend pushed. I pushed. Within a few months, people started commenting that I looked different, but I couldn't see it. Watching myself day in and day out, I couldn't see much change.

But eventually I did notice results. I wasn't getting sick anymore! An added benefit was that I was also getting bigger and stronger. It came slowly and felt so normal that I didn't see the transformation that was happening. It wasn't until I saw a picture of myself from a few months earlier that I realized something had changed. I had gained lots of muscle!

Spiritual disciplines work the same way. They work slowly. They aren't about willpower and overnight behavior modification. Spiritual disciplines are about God changing your desires and thoughts from a deep place within you. When you trust the process and practice the disciplines one day you'll realize you no longer struggle to control your anger. Self-control just becomes part of who you are. You don't have to drum up compassion, it just flows from you. You don't have to constantly fight a mental battle with lust or fear. Those thoughts just aren't there anymore. Responding like Jesus becomes second-nature, or rather, our new nature.

So what exactly are spiritual disciplines?

Spiritual disciplines are spiritual exercises that prepare us for God's transforming work in our lives. They strengthen us to walk in line with our new identity. Dallas Willard describes them as, "activities of the mind and body purposefully undertaken, to bring our personality and total being into effective cooperation with the divine order…" [22]

I learned to drive on narrow, country roads. I was always nervous about staying in the lines on the road. My dad taught me that, when you drive, you always move toward what you focus on. When you watch the lines, you'll move toward the lines. So, the secret is to choose a fixed point in the distance and watch it. Focus on that fixed point and you'll naturally stay in the lines.

Spiritual disciplines work the same way. They set God's truth as a fixed point in front of us. They bring who we really want to be to the forefront. When we focus on who we *aren't* and all the areas we need to change, we'll end up getting off track, driving over the lines. We'll live in condemnation. Spiritual disciplines give us a new focus. When we practice them, we move toward Christ's ideal and become who we really are. We change. We head to where we want to be. We become more like him.

DOING YOUR PART

The first part of this book was about identifying what holds you back. What comes next is a strategy for moving forward. This isn't some new way. It's an old way. G. K. Chesterton once said, "Christianity has not been tried and found wanting; it has been found difficult and not tried."[23] The disciplines I'm about to share are the solution for the problems we talked about in the first half of this book. They work, but they'll take work. They take discipline (thus the name!). But if you trust the process, they'll bring strength and freedom.

One note here: If you've read other books on spiritual disciplines and are thinking, *Oh, this again? I already know this,* I want you to forget what you think you know. Don't think in terms of obligation and duty and religion. Think in terms of end results. Think in terms of unlocking your potential. I know, I know. It feels selfish. *Can I really think about spiritual disciplines in terms of how they'll benefit me? Shouldn't this be about God?* But it's not selfish to embrace the purpose God has for you.

King David tells us to not forget about the benefits of getting in line with God's plan for us.[24] God's dreams for you are way bigger than the dreams you have for yourself. Few of us understand how much potential God has placed within us, but he knows. And he wants you to use that potential to the fullest. Everything God asks of you is for your good. Spiritual discipline is the way to give God's Spirit total freedom in your life. God gets the glory when he brings change. And when he gets the glory, we get joy. Put another way, we get the benefits. Peace. Confidence. Intimacy. Caring more about what God thinks than what other people think.

So what is the game plan for unlocking the power of all God says you really are? It's something I call the Freedom Triangle.

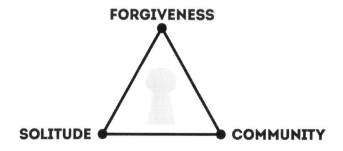

FORGIVENESS

SOLITUDE   **COMMUNITY**

When we practice forgiveness, solitude, and community together we walk in our true self in Christ. It takes all three parts. Practicing one or two corners may get you partial freedom. But Jesus came to give total freedom. Fortunately, he's the one who will complete the work.[25]

These three practices are where total transformation begins. So let's take a look at how you can get these disciplines working in your life.

CHAPTER 6

THE POWER OF FORGIVENESS

To be a Christian means to forgive the inexcusable, because God has forgiven the inexcusable in you.

—C.S. LEWIS

One of my bucket-list goals had always been

to sleep in a yurt, the round tents used by nomads, in Mongolia. During our second month in China, I decided it was now or never to go for it. This might be the closest I would ever get. So our team boarded a train and headed north on a section of the Trans-Siberian Railroad that goes from Beijing, into Mongolia, and ultimately crosses Russia. At around midnight we arrived at the border between China and Mongolia. We were told there'd be an extended stop for maintenance on the train, so we got off the train to explore the small town of Erlian.

Except for a few karaoke bars not much was open in the dusty border town on the edge of the Gobi Desert. So after about an hour I went back to the station. The rest of the team wanted to keep wandering around. When I got back to the station I was shocked to find that the train was already back and ready to leave! The conductor started blowing his air horn. The train attendants were frantically waving me onto the train. They were leaving. I had to stop that train! Using my massive vocabulary of thirteen Chinese words, I did my best to get the train to wait. It wasn't working. The train started moving forward. So I shoved our passports into the hands of an attendant, figuring he'd never leave us without them, and jumped off the train before he could hand them back. It was a gamble, but it was all I could think of. I bolted back into town to find the team. I was so focused on finding them that I ended up running through a slab of wet concrete!

After about ten minutes of ducking my head into every karaoke bar on the block I finally found them. I could hear the train at the station blowing its horn over and over. We sprinted through town and back to the train. Moments later we were rolling into Mongolia. Talk about a close call! My heart pounded for the next twenty minutes.

I often wonder what would have happened if that train had pulled into the night without us, leaving us in the middle of nowhere in China without passports…

So what was the reason for that train stop that nearly caused me to get stuck in the middle of nowhere? It was for a wheel change. They lifted up the entire train, removed the wheels, and then put on new ones. And why did they need to change the wheels? Well, back in the day, when Mongolia was controlled by the Soviet Union, the Chinese used different rail sizes to keep from being invaded by the Russians. It's only a three-inch difference between the two tracks, but if you don't change out those wheels, your train isn't crossing the border.

I've met people who seem to be stuck at a border in their lives. One experience—a hurt, an injustice, a betrayal, whatever—derailed their life, and they let that one experience define them. They can't let it go and it gets them stuck. Unforgiveness is the three-inch difference that will stop you in your tracks. But the decision to forgive is the change that allows you to keep moving forward.

MUDDIED WATERS

I took a Summit Leaders team rafting through the Grand Canyon a few years back. Our adventure started about two hours north of Flagstaff, Arizona. Where we started, the canyon is only a few hundred feet deep. The water is crystal clear with a nice green tint. You can see all the way to the bottom of the river. After a safety lesson, and a few basic paddling tips, we set out on our six-day journey deep into the canyon. But about two miles into the trip our guide pointed to the right. "Looks like the Paria is running," he said. "Say good-bye to the clear water."

I looked ahead and saw a nasty stream of brown water flowing into the crystal-clear Colorado River. In no time, our nice, clear river was brown and milky, and it stayed that way for the rest of the six-day trip. That one tiny, muddy seasonal stream miles upriver turned the mighty Colorado River into a cloudy mess.

King Solomon says, "Above all else, guard your heart, for everything you do flows from it."[1] Our hearts are meant to be pure and clear. That's part of our new identity. But if we aren't careful, hurt and bitterness will pollute that stream. One offense, betrayal, disappointment, or failure can taint the pure waters of our heart and leave us jaded.

When we don't release hurt it turns into resentment. In both Spanish and French the word *sentir* means *to feel.* When we re*sent* something we feel that emotion over and over. We relive the event. And resentment can have dire consequences, not only in our souls, but also in our bodies.

THE PRICE OF UNFORGIVENESS

A few years ago the church where I was working hired a homeless guy. He did great work, so we gave him a place to live and brought him on staff. He was prickly and had some paranoid tendencies, but slowly and surely he softened. He and I became friends and eventually he accepted Christ. He really wanted to please God, but he had a lot of hurt from his past. When things got difficult, he'd fall back into his old habits of anger and lashing out. Sometimes he'd disappear for a few days, then come back and apologize.

One day he showed up in my office hunched over, wincing. "I can't work today. My back flared up again. And I know why. It's because I won't forgive my sister. God is punishing me."

Clearly, this wasn't the time for a theological conversation about whether God causes pain or allows it. So I just asked him what he meant. He told me how his sister had hurt him. We talked about the power of forgiveness and he started to soften to the idea. But in a flash of anger he stood up. "I know God is punishing me for it. But I'm not letting her off the hook. She did too much to me!" He stormed out. He went to the doctor to get some pain meds, got back to work, and then we never talked about it again.

I'm not so sure about his theology that God was punishing him with pain, but based on what science has been uncovering about the negative power of unforgiveness there is a good possibility that the physical pain he experienced was connected in some way to his resentment.

Charlotte Witvliet, a professor at Hope College, asked seventy-one college students to either think about an injustice done to them or to think about forgiving someone who hurt them. She found that, "When focused on unforgiving responses, [the subjects'] blood pressure surged, their heart rates increased, brow muscles tensed, and negative feelings escalated." But, "by contrast, forgiving responses induced calmer feelings and physical responses." She concluded that "harboring unforgiveness comes at an emotional and a physiological cost. Cultivating forgiveness may cut these costs."[2]

Focusing on one thought, going over and over it in your mind, is called *ruminating.* The word *ruminate* has two meanings: 1) To think deeply about something, and 2) To bring up and chew again what has already been chewed and swallowed. Cows and sheep are ruminants. They keep eating the same food over and over again by chewing it, swallowing it, then heaving it back up into their mouth and chewing it some more. Yum, right?

Ruminating on hurt and negative thoughts is like chewing the same disgusting food over and over. In the words of one psychologist, "Rumination is the mental-health bad boy. It's associated with almost everything bad in the mental health field—obsessive-compulsive disorder, anxiety, depression ... probably hives too."[3]

Holding onto resentment and unforgiveness is like drinking poison and thinking the person who hurt you will die. You are the only one being hurt through unforgiveness.

THE FOUNDATION

Christianity is built on the conscious, willing act of one man taking on the sin of those who hurt him and choosing to not hold it against them. Jesus let us off the hook. He's our example of forgiveness.

True forgiveness isn't easy. In fact, at times it's downright hard. Just ask Jesus. At one point he begged, "Father, if you are willing, remove this cup from me. Nevertheless, not my will, but yours, be done."[4] If there was a way other than forgiveness it seems like Jesus would have gladly taken it. You know the emotional pain and guilt you carry from your own failures and how people have hurt you. Can you imagine what it would be like to carry that kind of weight for every person who has ever lived?

Jesus took the hard road of forgiveness because he knew it was God's will for him and for the world. It was an act of obedience. "He learned obedience through what he suffered."[5] Jesus forgave and he tells us "now go and do the same."[6] The journey to embracing your true self requires forgiving others and yourself. Not just once, but over and over and over.

When Peter asked how many times he had to forgive someone who hurt him, Jesus told the story of a man who owed a huge debt to a king. There was no way he could ever pay that debt, so he begged for mercy. The king forgave the man's entire debt, just because he asked. But right after the man who had been forgiven the huge debt left the palace he ran into someone who owed him a tiny amount of money. Apparently, the guy had short-term memory loss and forgot how much he had just been forgiven. He started to choke the man who owed him money and sent him to prison for failure to pay. Word got back to the king about what had happened, so the king called the man back into his palace. He was furious. "You wicked servant," he said, "I canceled all that debt of yours because you begged me to. Shouldn't you have had mercy on your fellow servant just as I had on you?"

Then the king handed that man who wouldn't forgive over to jailers to be tortured. If the story wasn't intense enough, Jesus drives the point of his story home by explaining, "This is how my heavenly Father will treat each of you unless you forgive your brother or sister from your heart."[7] Resentment can feel like torture. And God won't remove those feelings if we choose to not forgive. Bottom line of the story: Forgiveness isn't optional for Christians. And, as with everything God asks of us, forgiveness *is* good for us. It frees us from the pain of living with past hurt.

RELEASING CONTROL

Several years ago I was deeply hurt by a pastor I worked for. I knew I needed to forgive him. I talked it through with a counselor. I said I forgave him. I did my best to forget about it. But deep down I felt that if I completely let it go I would be allowing him to get away with what he did to me. That went against every sense of justice within me. Looking back, I realize that I was upset that God would forgive him. In my mind, that pastor didn't deserve it. When I got honest, I realized I was being that unforgiving servant Jesus talked about in the parable. I didn't trust God to bring justice. So I was trying to take justice into my hands.

For several months I hung on to resentment against him for what he had done. It wasn't a good feeling, but I just kept wallowing in misery. I felt trapped and helpless. Day after day I would whine and complain about the horrible things that pastor had done to me and my family. I was stuck.

It took me longer than it should have, but I eventually decided to release this man from the prison I thought I had put him in. The thing is, *I* was the one in prison. The moment I truly forgave and let it go, a newfound optimism and hope started stirring in me. It was like a fog of depression lifted. I started to look at all the possibilities in front of me.

It was only a few days after that decision to forgive that I sat down and, in about ten days, wrote an entire book! That was the first of my books to be published. I believe there was a direct correlation between choosing to forgive and God giving me a desire of my heart. Writing that book launched me into what I'm doing today as a personal development coach, writer, and speaker. But to get to that place, I had to let go of past hurt. The same is true in your life.

To move forward you must let it go and forgive.

PASSING THE TEST

Someone once said that getting over a painful experience is like crossing monkey bars: you have to let go at some point to move forward. Forgiveness is often the test that God uses to see if you are ready for the next level in your life.

Test?

Yes, God tests us.

God never does evil to us, but he allows evil to be used for his purposes. He allows challenges into our life to test us. It would be easy to think that God is doing something mean by testing us. But he has every right in the universe to do this. Like that king, he forgave our huge debt. We deserve nothing. Nothing. But God is overflowing with grace and gives us wonderful blessings. But he isn't going to give you something you aren't ready for. He has a destiny for you and he knows what it'll take to get you there. So he tests and prepares us, for our good. God never gives up on us. Even if you don't get it right the first time, he'll let you keep taking the test over and over until you're refined and ready for the good things he has ahead for you. (But if you can, pass the test the first time so you don't have to do a retake.) Your destiny depends on you learning to forgive!

Nelson Mandela spent twenty-seven years of his life in prison under South African apartheid. That's over one-fourth of his life spent in prison. What's more, his imprisonment was entirely unjust. Fortunately for the world, he understood the power and importance of forgiveness. He said, "As I walked out the door toward the gate that would lead to my freedom, I knew if I didn't leave my bitterness and hatred behind, I'd still be in prison."[8] He eventually became President of South Africa. Instead of using that power to get back at people who had wronged him, he brought unity to a country that was deeply divided. He became a symbol of reconciliation around the world. What happened to Nelson Mandela was unjust and wrong, but his decision to forgive was an example to an entire nation of how to rise higher and move forward. Your decision to forgive can do the same. It can be an example to those around you.

THE MYTHS OF FORGIVENESS

One of the most common statements I hear when working with people who are having a hard time forgiving is: "But the person who hurt me needs to apologize before I forgive them. They need to admit their guilt."

This is where Jesus's example of forgiveness is so powerful. As he hung on the cross, right in the middle of an act of betrayal by the very people he came to help, he said, "Father forgive them for they do not know what they are doing."[9] Jesus forgave before we ever asked for it. I'm convinced this is the model for true forgiveness. We need to forgive before those who hurt us even know that they're being forgiven. We simply release them, whether they ask for forgiveness or not.

You may never hear an apology from the person who hurt you. They may never admit guilt. If the person who hurt you is a parent who has passed away, or a criminal who was never caught, it isn't possible to seek a confession. In many cases, it's dangerous and unwise to confront the person who hurt you.

The great news is, you don't need the other person to acknowledge their guilt before you can forgive them. The power to forgive is in your hands, right here and now. Remember, living from the true self always starts from the inside and works its way out. Being a forgiving person is part of your new identity in Christ. Your true self is a forgiving person because God gives you grace to forgive, if you'll just take it. Even if circumstances or your environment don't change, you can walk in the freedom of forgiveness.

Here's another myth of forgiveness. "I'll forgive when it feels right." I hate to break it to you, but that good feeling will probably never come. But forgiveness doesn't come as a result of some mystical good feeling. Instead, it's the opposite. The good feeling of forgiveness will only come after you *choose* to forgive and keep reminding yourself of your decision.

When you make a decision to forgive, it's done. You've forgiven. Now you just live it out, even if your feelings haven't caught up. It's not that you fake it until you make it, it's more a conscious decision to embrace the reality that you are a forgiving person in Christ, your true self. So you walk in ongoing forgiveness.

The final myth of forgiveness is a line most of us have heard so many times that we don't even realize how flawed it is. The myth is this: Forgive and forget.

Let me be blunt: you cannot forgive and forget. It's impossible. Your mind is too powerful to just forget. It always remembers. If you spend your life trying to forget something someone did to you, thinking this is true forgiveness, you'll live in constant guilt. We don't forgive and forget, we forgive and choose to remember with forgiveness.

IN THE TRENCHES OF FORGIVENESS

Forgiveness is a decision. You don't need to have any warm fuzzy feelings before you forgive. You don't have to wait for a certain amount of time to pass. You just decide: I'm going to forgive. So let me offer some practical steps to help you through his decision.

Forgiveness starts by admitting, "I was hurt."

That's hard to admit, especially if you see yourself as a strong person. Admitting we got hurt makes us feel vulnerable. But once you get up the courage to admit you were hurt, you've cracked open the door to be able to forgive.

The next step is to admit *how* you were hurt. You have to actually name the hurt and shame. *I was betrayed. I was lied to. I was abandoned. I was rejected.* You need to say it out loud to your-

> *We don't forgive and forget, we forgive and choose to remember with forgiveness.*

self. If you want, you can use the following as an example of what to say:

- *Name of person* betrayed my trust and used it to take advantage of me. He hurt me.

- *Name of person* lied to me and then told lies about me. She hurt me.

- *Name of person* betrayed my family's trust. He hurt my family.

- *Name of person* abandoned me. The person who should have protected me left me alone.

This is an intense process, so I don't recommend doing it alone. Ask a pastor or professional counselor who understands forgiveness to walk through it with you. When I chose to forgive that pastor, my friend and counselor Catherine helped me walk through it.

Admitting hurt involves grieving, which we'll address in more detail in the next section. It's enough here to say grieving can be painful. We have to recognize what we lost. We have to express our sadness over the loss, which can be painful. Which is why many people decide they don't want to take this step. But trust me, the cost of holding onto the hurt is far worse than the temporary pain of confessing and grieving it.

After I confessed my hurt and what I lost, Catherine told me to repeat the ways that pastor had hurt me, but she had me add one final statement at the end: "But I choose to forgive him for hurting me."

It was awkward to say it all out loud again. But the relief I felt was amazing. It was like I regained a sense of hope and perspective. I wasn't a victim. I was choosing to forgive someone who had hurt me. It was my choice. More important, I was embracing God's grace to forgive and that released peace in my life.

And then there's one final step: You have to remind yourself of your decision. Remind yourself when you wake up. Remind yourself when you think about what the person did. Remind yourself before you go to bed. You'll know you've truly forgiven when you look back at the hurt and feel no anger—only peace.

Forgiveness always leads to inner peace. A deep peace that goes beyond understanding.

THE SPIRAL OF FORGIVENESS

Forgiveness involves grieving. You've probably heard of the five stages of grief: denial, anger, bargaining, depression, and acceptance. Because they're called *stages*, it's easy to think grief is a linear process. Stage 1, 2, 3…Click. *Yeah! I'm over it!* But grieving isn't like that. It's more like a spiral. The pain tends to loop back around. You may wake up days, months, or years later and be hit by a wave of sadness and anger that feels just as intense as the moment the hurt happened. This doesn't mean you haven't truly forgiven. It just means you need to remind yourself that you chose to forgive. The good news is, the spiral will get wider and wider. The episodes will get further and further apart. If the spiral comes back around again, don't feel guilty. It's normal. Just remind yourself that you chose to forgive. Eventually you'll get to a place where the memory of the event will only bring peace.

SET YOURSELF FREE RIGHT NOW

So let me ask you something: Who do you need to forgive? What past hurts or events are holding you back from being totally free? If there are memories that you still don't have peace or resolution about, maybe it's time to forgive and move on.

Don't just sit around and hope the hurt will go away. It won't. You have to be proactive about it. Explore the hurt. Acknowledge what it did to you, no matter how long ago it was. Surrender the hurt and decide to forgive that person and release them from what they did to you.

And here's the really big question: What about forgiving yourself? Have you ever looked at how you've hurt yourself? Sure, you probably live with it every day, but have you ever actually identified and named it? I'd encourage you to do so. Give it a name and then ask God for forgiveness. The moment you ask, he'll forgive you. And then ask him to help you forgive yourself. Never forget that God forgave you, so you have no right to not forgive yourself.

Never forget that God forgave you, so you have no right to not forgive yourself.

Make it your goal to be a person who walks in ongoing forgiveness. Get your life back on track. Embrace your new identity as a person who forgives. Then move forward with confidence into the wide-open spaces of all God has for you.

CHAPTER 7

THE STRENGTH IN SOLITUDE

Without solitude it is virtually impossible to live a spiritual life. Solitude begins with a time and place for God, and for him alone. If we really believe not only that God exists but also that he is actively present in our lives—healing, teaching, and guiding—we need to set aside a time and space to give him our undivided attention.

—HENRI NOUWEN

The quietest place I've ever been was near the Rombuk Glacier at the foot of Mt. Everest. The silence there was so complete that it was actually a bit eerie.

It took us nearly two full days to drive through the Tibetan highlands from Lhasa to Qomolongma, the local name for Mt. Everest. My head was pounding most of the trip as we crossed 16,000-ft passes and drove long stretches at altitudes above 14,000 ft. We arrived at the foot of Mt. Everest just before sunset on the second day. We unloaded our gear into a Buddhist monastery, supposedly the highest monastery in the world, which had a special section for housing travelers. I'll never forget looking back over my shoulder as I brought our gear into the monastery. The clouds had cleared and I could see the summit of Mt. Everest, 29,029 feet above sea level. The setting sun created an orange alpenglow on the snow-capped peak. I remember thinking, *That summit is two miles higher than where I am now and I am absolutely miserable. I never want to climb that beast!*

Dinner was yak-meat stew and bread. I hardly ate anything because the altitude had killed my appetite. That night was so cold that my water bottle actually froze inside my room in the monastery. Between the cold, my pounding headache, and regular trips to the outhouse from all the water I was drinking to stay hydrated, I didn't get much sleep. But the sun eventually rose and it was time to hike toward Everest.

We walked right past a sign warning us that we would be fined $20,000 U.S. Dollars for crossing that point without the proper permit… The farther we hiked, the more our team spread out. At one point I looked up and realized I was all alone, standing next to a giant sheet of ice. Seconds later the sun cleared the peak just behind me. The warmth was a relief, so I laid down on a rock. I listened.

Total silence. Total stillness. Total solitude.

From time to time, I'd hear the crack of ice somewhere around me as the sun did its best to melt the permafrost. But other than that, it was absolutely silent. I'm not sure I've had that much silence since.

Even though it was quiet all around me, inside my head it was chaos. My brain was on overdrive sorting through upcoming travel plans, money concerns, and what it would be like when I got home. It was hard to enjoy the moment because I just couldn't get my mind to shut off.

I'm guessing you can relate. Even if you manage to find a quiet place or moment, getting your mind to calm down is a whole other challenge. Finding solitude and calm is hard, but it's a skill that anyone can learn with a little practice.

THE POWER OF SOLITARY PRACTICE

Your mind is like a powerful super-computer with unlimited memory. Many scientists believe that the mind never forgets anything, it just stores it. At any given moment we can access memories hiding deep in our subconscious. This can be a gift, but it can also be a struggle. It's far too easy for our mind to be filled with negative thoughts and anxiety, rather than the truth of who God says you are in Christ.

Solitude is the key to getting your mind under control.

In Isaiah 30:15, God tells Israel, "In repentance and rest is your salvation, in quietness and trust is your strength." At first glance, this verse seems counterintuitive. Strength usually comes from exertion. When you want to build strength, you create resistance against your muscles. You push and stretch. No pain, no gain. But God says that spiritual strength comes from quietness and trust.

Anders Ericsson is a psychologist who has spent lots of time researching what makes people an expert in any given field. He concluded that to become an expert it takes 10,000 hours of practice in your field. But not just any practice. He says experts use something called *deliberate practice.* In his book *Peak,* he talks about a study that tried to figure out what set apart the best of the best. In one study of top-tier violin students, researchers found that the primary difference between the best and the best of the best was "the total number of hours devoted to solitary practice."[1] Essentially, Ericsson says, the ones who rise to the very top are those who spend focused time on their own, developing strength in their field through practice.

This applies to our spiritual life too. There is a level of growth in your life that will never happen around others. If you want to fully embrace who God says you are, you must take focused time away. Alone. In quietness and trust.

Solitude (quietness and trust) is the deliberate practice of those who are determined to live in their true self.

WHEN THE NOISE STOPS

Ever noticed how noise drives more noise? You arrive at a restaurant and there are only a handful of people. Slowly, as more people arrive, the noise level goes up. Dishes rattling, people talking, and that one person with a ridiculously loud laugh. Before long you're nearly yelling to talk to someone just across the table. Add the ambient music, and you've got a steady hum of noise. Even if the noise stops for a moment, the music fills the gaps.

When I was a worship leader I had all the musicians stop playing for a few moments every Sunday and we'd just have a time of total silence. When we got a new pastor he called me in one day and told me to stop doing the time of silence because it made people feel uncomfortable. I didn't agree with his decision, but he was reflecting how most people feel about silence. It's uncomfortable. When the noise shuts off, we have to face our thoughts, fears, and insecurity. So we keep the noise going, ignore what's happening just beneath the surface within us, and wonder why we're in a constant state of anxiety and stress.

When the noise shuts off, we have to face our thoughts, fears, and insecurity.

In 2013, Imke Kirste, a regenerative biologist from Duke University, studied how sounds affect the brains of adult mice. Four different groups of mice were exposed to various sounds: music, baby mouse calls, white noise, and silence. All the different sounds had some short-term effect on the brains of the mice. But she was amazed to discover, "that two hours of silence per day prompted cell development in the hippocampus…The total absence of input was having a more pronounced effect than any sort of input tested." After doing more tests to explore the results she concluded, "Silence is really helping the new generated cells to differentiate into neurons, and integrate into the system."[2]

Silence builds the brain. It has a life-giving effect on our bodies and minds.

THE VOICE YOU WANT TO HEAR

In my coaching program, one of the most common statements I hear from people who are in a transition is, "I just wish God would speak to me and tell me what to do." They want an angel to appear or a hand to write in the sky. I understand, I'd like that too!

But remember how God spoke to Elijah? He appeared as a powerful wind and then an earthquake. But after all that passed, God spoke in *the sound of a low whisper.*[3] When God speaks to his children, he tends to do it gently. Quietly.

We all want to know God's will for our life. We want a clear, loud voice from on high to tell us what to do. But I'm pretty certain that would scare most of us. The Bible has stories of God speaking out loud.[4] But typically, when God speaks loudly it's to pronounce judgment or make a declaration. When he wants to guide us he tends to go with a whisper.

He is always speaking, it's up to us to get quiet enough to listen and pay attention to his voice.

Richard Foster says, "One reason we can hardly bear to remain silent is that it makes us feel so helpless. We are so accustomed to relying upon words to manage and control others…The tongue is our most powerful weapon of manipulation."[5]

A while back, Emily and I went to visit some of her relatives in The Netherlands. I'm an introvert, but I'm pretty good around new people. I tell jokes and try to make people feel comfortable, and hopefully make them like me. But her relatives didn't speak English, so all my talking skills didn't work. And I'm a horrible mime. So, there were lots of moments of silence, sitting around and staring at each other. Awkward. I started to realize just how much I depend on words to win people over, trying to get their approval. It's part of my false self. But in this situation, I was helpless. The silence forced me to give up a sense of control over the conversation.

This talking habit of mine carries over into my times with God. I tend to rumble into my "quiet time" by firing off a list of requests and grievances. It's 99% talk, 1% listening. Paul tells us to "not by anxious about anything, but in every situation, by prayer and petition, with thanksgiving, present your request to God."[6] We like the presenting part. It helps us feel like something is getting done. So we fill the airwaves with requests. But it's really hard to hear when you are talking all the time. Sure, present your requests to God, but be sure you are leaving space for God to talk back. Leave space to hear his voice.

THE PRACTICE OF SOLITUDE

Unless you are living in a monastery or in a tent in the Rocky Mountains, I'm guessing that right about now you're thinking, *How on earth will I ever find solitude?* We've got jobs, bills to pay, yelling kids to care for, relationships that require maintenance. You may not have the luxury of spending hours on end in nature or silence, but you can create small moments of solitude and silence right where you are. You just have to be intentional about it. Here are some practical steps you can take to practice solitude in your life:

1 — MAKE IT A PRIORITY

Carve out a time and place for solitude. Set a non-optional appointment with God. If you are just trying to slip solitude into your life, it will never happen. It has to be scheduled. This means you might have to drop one or two things, or it might mean you'll need to get to bed or wake up a little earlier. You also need to choose a place that's conducive to silence. An attorney in my coaching program started packing his lunch rather than going out. He'd eat, then he'd slip into a church near his work and spend time in prayer over lunch. He started to really look forward to those midday times with God.

You may not have the luxury of getting out of the house or office. But there are still opportunities. Drive to work with the radio off. Get to work a little early and just sit in your car silently. Or choose a chair or corner in your

If you are just trying to slip solitude into your life, it will never happen. It has to be scheduled.

house that will be your place. Make it a sacred place. Let everyone know: "Unless you are dying, don't disturb me when I'm in this corner."

2 — SET A REALISTIC, ATTAINABLE GOAL

When you accomplish small goals, you build momentum. You start to see that bigger goals are possible. I've set way too many lofty prayer goals. *"I'm going to pray for thirty minutes per day!"* I pull it off for two days, then I miss a day. I feel guilty and figure I'll make it up the following day. I rarely do. Instead I just give up on praying all together. Don't do that!

Give yourself a fighting chance. Start with something reasonable and small. Five to ten dedicated minutes of total attention to quietness. Just see how it goes. Small steps and little victories will help you build momentum in your prayer life.

3 — SILENCE THE MONKEYS

Once you stop and get quiet, the next challenge is what Henri Nouwen describes as "calming the monkeys jumping in the banana trees." A few years back, one of my adventure teams camped in the jungle ruins of Yaxha, an unexcavated Mayan city. A family of howler monkeys was pretty upset about us being there. They groaned and screamed for hours. It wasn't until late in the night that they finally calmed down and we were able to get some peace and quiet.

When you start to practice solitude, there will probably be some "monkeys" howling in your head. Upcoming obligations. Work responsibilities. Worries about family. Keep a pen handy to write down items you need to remember. Once you've written them down, put them out of your mind and get back to silence. If you're serious about it, the monkeys will eventually quiet down. It gets easier over time.

Once you've set a time, place, and managed to calm the noise in your head, there are several spiritual disciplines you can use to give space for God to do his work in your heart.

MEDITATION

As a kid I was told that meditation was *new age* and that it opened the door to evil spirits. Being possessed by evil spirits has never been on my bucket list, so I avoided meditation. All these warnings seemed to be confirmed years later when I visited a Tibetan Buddhist monastery in the Himalayas. Listening to their droning mantras was a creepy feeling. Yup, no thanks on the meditation.

But eventually I learned that meditation is a *Christian* practice. Christ-followers have been using meditation for 2,000 years, and it's not something to be feared. In fact, it's a tried-and-true method to connect with God.

I like Richard Foster's simple definition of meditation: "Christian meditation, very simply, is the ability to hear God's voice and obey."[7]

In Eastern meditation the goal is to empty your mind, to become an empty vessel. Christian meditation is about filling your mind with truth straight from the mind of God.

King David says that when we meditate on God's word we are like a, "tree planted by streams of water that yields its fruit in its season, and its leaf does not wither. In all that he does, he prospers…"[8]

If meditation sounds awkward and uncomfortable, let me give you some reassurance. You already know how to do this. You did it last night at 2:00 a.m. when you were awake, worried about the layoffs at work. You did it when you thought all day about the conflict in your marriage. Most of us are world-class worriers. So meditation should come easy. If you can worry, you can meditate. It's the same process.

And actually, meditation is the cure for worry. It's ruminating, but it's ruminating on truth. It's chewing on truths about who God is and who he says we are until those truths are absorbed into our minds and hearts. And that truth brings calm and peace.

> *If you can worry, you can meditate. It's the same process.*

WHAT ONLY GOD CAN DO

Jared was serving in the military when he joined my coaching program. Several years earlier he had a pretty traumatic deployment to Afghanistan. Since that time, he struggled with insomnia. He tried doctors, counselors, and pills to get relief. Nothing worked. Eventually he just resigned himself to the fact that he'd probably always struggle with sleep.

I didn't know he had this problem, but in the program we talk about mediating on Scripture. He started meditating in the morning and found it calmed his mind for the day. So he decided to meditate on Scripture right before bed rather than watch TV or read.

Then something incredible happened.

For the first time in years, he was able to sleep through the night.

Meditation did what doctors, counselors, and pills couldn't! When he called to tell me this amazing news, it immediately reminded me of Isaiah 26:3: "You keep him in perfect peace whose mind is stayed on you, because he trusts in you." Meditation helped Jared conquer anxiety and post-traumatic stress. God can do anything. *Anything.* He can heal, restore, and bring peace. His truth is unstoppable when we let it run wild in our minds and hearts.

ST. PAUL'S SCHOOL OF SELF-HELP

Self-help gurus rave about the power of speaking affirmations to yourself throughout the day and before you sleep.

"I'm the smartest person I know. I attract good things into my life. People like me."

I used to laugh at this as self-absorbed and ridiculous. You can't just make something up that you want to be true about yourself, say it a bunch of times, and have it become reality. That's a magic spell.

But I know lots of people who had their life changed through affirmations. So maybe there's something to it, if it's based on the right foundation. Paul tells us in Romans 12:2 to not be conformed to the world but to be transformed by the renewing of the mind. Essentially, he's telling us to stop thinking like the world and start thinking the way God does. To make God's thoughts your thoughts. Reprogram your mind with a new reality.

Meditating day and night sounds a whole lot like repeating those self-help affirmations. The more you repeat it, the more your brain believes it. But there's one big difference between affirmations and meditation: the word of God isn't about self-focused, gimmie-gimmie affirmations—it's about absolute, unchanging truth. It's God's thoughts. When we meditate on the inspired, unchanging word of God, we can't go wrong. When we tell our minds what *he* thinks about us, we start to think like he does.

Surely, goodness and mercy will follow me all the days of my life.

In all things I am more than a conqueror.

God always leads me in victorious triumph.

My God will supply all my needs according to his riches.

I am the righteousness of God in Christ.[9]

That's all truth straight from the mind of God. What God says will always stay true.[10] It's as true today as when it was written. It's the unchanging truth that will change us—once it's in us.

Now, take the next logical step. When God spoke his first recorded words, "Let there be light," the universe was created. He spoke it and it was. That's real, ultimate power. Scientists and most Christians agree that the universe is still expanding. The first creative words God spoke are still creating, widening the known universe. Is it possible, then, that when we speak his words out loud they still hold the power to create and expand our world? Absolutely!

We expand our world when we unleash his truth into it. Our thoughts get bigger. We grow. His words tear down our walls and lead us out into the wide-open spaces of his plans for us.

It's one thing to *think* about God's truth, but sometimes we need to meditate on it out loud. King David encouraged himself in the Lord when he was down. "Why are you cast down, O my soul, and why are you in turmoil within me? Hope in God; for I shall again praise him, my salvation and my God.[11] David wasn't known to hold back. (At one point, his dancing got so aggressive that his clothes started coming off![12]) I don't think it's a stretch to bet that David reminded himself of God's truth in a loud voice. Sometimes our meditation needs to get loud.

STUDY

In school I got really good at cramming for tests. I never paid attention in class because I knew I could learn what I needed the night before the test. This worked well until the final exam came along and I had forgotten everything I'd crammed in my head earlier in the semester.

It's the same in our spiritual walk. If we only cram truth into our minds when we are in a jam, we can't expect lasting transformation. Real study makes us internalize and incorporate what we learn and memorize.

Meditation and study go hand in hand. When we study God's word, his word studies us. When we study God's truth we're really saying, "Search me, O God, and know my heart."[14]

Study is vital when it comes to discerning between our true and false self. The soul and spirit are closely connected. Sometimes our emotions, thoughts, and desires are so strong that they feel true. When your body is tired or you feel overwhelmed, your emotions can lead you to do all sorts of crazy. What you feel in your soul can seem so real and certain that you may even think it's God telling you to do it. I've had people tell me they were certain God was telling them, deep inside their heart, to leave their kids and run off with someone they met on the internet. They even got goose bumps when they prayed about it. They were certain it was God's will. They were sincere.

When we study God's word, his word studies us.

Sincerely wrong.

God's word helps us avoid self-deception. That's what Paul is talking about when he says, "the word of God is living and active, sharper than any two-edged sword, piercing to the division of soul and of spirit, of joints and of marrow, and discerning the thoughts and intentions of the heart."[15] You have to study God's truth, inside and out, to make sure you aren't getting confused about what's God's spirit and what's just the desires of your old, false self. The foundation for practicing the spiritual discipline of study should always be God's word. Never stop studying the Bible.

Another great area of study is the stories of believers who have gone before us. We're surrounded by a great "cloud of witnesses"[16] who have walked with God through good and bad. When we learn about God's work in their lives, he'll often teach us powerful principles we can incorporate into our lives. Read biographies of great men and women of God. Study his work throughout history. We aren't the first ones trying to navigate this crazy world. Learn from those who have gone before us.

God also speaks to us as we study our memories. God has been writing a story with your life through the good, bad, and ugly. But we usually don't see that while it's happening. As Kierkegaard said, "Life is lived forward. But it can only be understood looking backward." When we study God's work in our life, we build our faith to see that he is transforming us and redeeming our story. Frederick Buechner talks about the power of studying your life when he says:

> *"Listen to your life. See it for the fathomless mystery it is. In the boredom and pain of it, no less than in the excitement and gladness: touch, taste, smell your way to the holy and hidden heart of it, because in the last analysis all moments are key moments, and life itself is grace."*[17]

God is always at work in your life. There are some experiences in life we won't understand on this side of eternity, but there are others that God wants to use to bring a deep sense of purpose and calling to your life. Study God's work in your life and you'll begin to see his redemption.

As you study and explore God's work in your life, there's a good chance you'll begin to see glimpses of the huge work he is doing. You'll see just how far he brought you. You'll see how he has been preparing you for your next step. God wastes nothing. He wants to redeem everything that has happened to you and use it to tell the story of his glory in your life. Your next step will be in line with what God has been doing over the years. Everything that has happened to you is something God wants to use in your next season of life. Study his work in your life, and you'll find your purpose.

SECRECY

We all want approval. We want to be accepted and recognized. But looking for approval can get out of hand in a hurry. We are all prone to get addicted to approval. It's a swirling vortex that sucks us in before we even realize it. When you live for the approval and acceptance of others you will always be disappointed. The approval we really need only comes from God.

Enter secrecy.

This discipline is the number-one key to breaking our approval addiction. It's something we could all use a little more of in this approval-driven world. In the spiritual discipline of secrecy, we do good and don't tell anyone about it.

I like to believe that I don't need approval from people, but I do. When the offering plate comes by in

He wants to redeem everything that has happened to you and use it to tell the story of his glory in your life.

church and I don't drop anything in, I'll sometimes mumble, "Yup, I already gave online." I don't want Mrs. Ramirez to think I'm not a giver. What she thinks of me matters.

Too much.

Secrecy is the cure for this approval addiction. Lots of people do good stuff trying to get recognition, but only the truly strong are willing to do good alone, in obscurity, without needing to announce to the world what they've done. In Matthew 6, Jesus says to do our good works "in secret."

As usual with God, obedience has its benefits. He promises that "your Father who sees in secret will reward you."[18]

I'm probably gonna step on some toes here, but I feel like we're friends now, so I'll just say it: I'm concerned about how we use social media to publicize sacred parts of our life, like time in solitude. #morningdevo #jesusismycoffee-date #growinginChrist. My discomfort hits another level when I see people posting as they help the less fortunate. #peopleneedtheLord #Haitimissiontrip.

I don't want to be a buzzkill. Sharing your life is fun. And I don't want to get all legalistic about it. So you and Jesus need to figure out what obedience in secrecy looks like in your life. Posting things online can inspire others to get involved in serving and spending time with God, but I don't want us to miss out on part of the reward of those acts by choosing to document it all through photos and videos. I also wonder if doing this on social media is feeding our false self and our approval addiction.

Not sure you've got an approval addiction? Here's a simple test: Post a picture on social media and then don't look at who liked it for three days. If me just suggesting this shot a surge of anxiety through your chest, then there's your sign. But seriously. Can you do it? If not, you might have approval addiction. Keep a close eye on your motives when posting things on social media or doing acts of service to others.

Secrecy is a form of self-denial, which is a pre-requisite for following Jesus.[19] It's like fasting (another spiritual discipline you should explore), but instead of denying yourself food, you are denying yourself recognition. God's recognition is all we need. God works humility into us when we decide that his approval is enough. We get the benefit of God's Spirit working quietly within us. We get confidence.

SERIOUS ABOUT SOLITUDE

For you to unlock all that God says you are, you'll have to get really familiar with solitude. You'll have to get serious about getting away from the noise and the crowd for a one-on-one encounter with God. Listen for his still, small whisper. No group Bible study, fellowship, or Sunday sermon can make up for focused time in solitude. You can't get where you want to be without it. It's the stuff that nobody sees, what you do in solitude, that brings the results everyone wants.

CHAPTER 8

THE LIFE OF COMMUNITY

No man is an island, entire of itself; every man is a piece of the continent, a part of the main. —JOHN DONNE

The final part of my four-month China adventure had arrived. We boarded a plane headed to Guangzhou, China, right near the border with Hong Kong. I was relieved when I finally got to my aisle-seat, but I was also annoyed with myself because they had confiscated my favorite knife at security. I forgot it was in my carry-on. It crossed China with me, but got taken on the final leg of my journey! I sat down and closed my eyes, hoping to sleep a little.

But within seconds of sitting down, a young Chinese man next to me began touching my watch. I pulled my hand away.

In broken English he asked, "Are you American?"

I confirmed that I was.

"How much cost the watch?"

I sighed, knowing where this was going.

Cultural fatigue was taking its toll at this point. The lack of personal space and boundaries in China was starting to wear on me. Even before Communism, China was a communal society. People shared and did everything together. The community always took precedence over individualism. Asking very personal and intrusive questions is normal. Add to that cultural element the fact that I had been traveling around Asia with the same people for four months and I'm an introvert. I was exhausted.

I loved the people I was with, but we still got on each other's nerves. We knew each other's idiosyncrasies. We irritated each other. We laughed together and got frustrated with each other. At this point in the journey, we were all tired of being in such close quarters day in and day out. But looking back, this closeness was part of the foundation for the work God had been doing in my heart during my time in China.

There is something we individualistic Westerners can learn from tightknit, communal societies: God uses community to help us learn who we really are. To find our place.

And there's nothing like community to reveal what's really inside of you.

THE RELATIONSHIPS THAT HEAL

One of the big mantras of counseling is, "It's the relationship that heals." Building a trusting relationship with the person sitting in front of you is way more important than any skills or training you get. Healing comes from the relationships we have with others. This means you don't need counseling skills to help others get over their hang-ups. You just need to have a loving relationships with them.

We're wired for connection. Think back to the Garden of Eden. Adam had direct connection to his Creator, but God knew people need other people. So he made Eve. When Adam and Eve severed their connection with God, sin severed their connection with each other. Not long after sin entered the world we see the strained relationship between Cain and his brother Abel.

When we're separated from God, we're separated from others.

Fortunately, through Christ our relationship with God was restored. Which means our relationship with others can now be restored. We can connect with others in a life-giving way because we are connected to the source of life—Jesus. It's in this connection with others that God helps us come out from behind our false self and embrace who he says we really are. You cannot become fully you apart from community. It's a strange irony of God's ways that it's people who hurt us, but it's also people that God uses to bring healing.

LOVING GOD ISN'T ENOUGH

A guy once asked Jesus what was the most important command God had given. He wanted the bottom line. But Jesus gave two bottom lines. "You shall love the Lord your God with all your heart and with all your soul and with all your mind. This is the great and first commandment. And a second is like it: You shall love your neighbor as yourself."[1] Oh, how I wish God had just said, "Love me." I can do that most of the time. But he didn't. He said that loving people is an extension of loving God. You cannot truly love God if you don't love and connect with people.

John reiterates this when he says, "he who does not love his brother, whom he has seen, cannot love God, whom he has not seen."[2] Our relationship with others is the barometer for our love for God. You and Jesus may have it all worked out, but it's how you live with those around you that proves it.

Being alone with Jesus in solitude is the foundation for transformation. But it doesn't end there. We need a balance of being alone and being with others—solitude and community. Dietrich Bonhoeffer says it this way:

> *"Let him who cannot be alone beware of community... Let him who is not in community beware of being alone... Each by itself has profound perils and pitfalls. One who wants fellowship without solitude plunges into the void of words and feelings, and the one who seeks solitude without fellowship perishes in the abyss of vanity, self-infatuation, and despair."*[3]

Healthy community starts when each member of the community spends time in solitude with God. It's like recharging your batteries so you can infuse more life into those around you. You've probably heard a preflight safety announcement tell you, in an emergency, to "put on your oxygen mask first, then assist others." Makes sense. If you're short on oxygen you won't be able to help anyone else. Solitude keeps us strong so we can bring life to others in our community.

In healthy community, everyone is pulling their own spiritual weight, spending time with God on their own, bringing that life back into the community for everyone's benefit. Sure, there are seasons (sometimes long seasons) when some can't pull their weight. Tragedy, illness, or discouragement hit them hard. They need extra care. That's what community is for, to care for one another. We invest in those who are hurting to bring them back to a place of strength, so they, in turn, can help others.

You and Jesus may have it all worked out, but it's how you live with those around you that proves it.

Over the years I've known people who seemed to suck the life out of me. You can probably name a few in your own life. There's no mutual encouragement. It's just them taking. That is unhealthy community. When members of community always take and never give, that's dysfunctional. Typically, the issue is that those people aren't spending their own time in solitude. They're looking for the community to bring something only God can bring. This happens in lots of marriages. We look to our spouse to fulfill something only God can. We're perpetually annoyed at our spouse, looking for them to give us something they just can't give.

Henri Nouwen talked about the importance of being *wounded healers*. Hang around with people for more than a day and you'll get hurt—even in healthy community. We're all in recovery from our false self, so we unintentionally hurt others. But the irony is that our woundedness equips us to bring healing to others. It gives us compassion and understanding.

Alcoholics Anonymous, which I'll talk more about in a moment, is a group of wounded healers. It's folks who got honest about how little control they had over alcohol, and who looked to others who shared the same woundedness to be support in the struggle.

We all want to hide our wounds. That's a natural part of our shame-based defenses. But as long as we hide our wounds, we can't be healed of them.

WHAT THEY DON'T SEE CAN'T HURT THEM, RIGHT?

When I worked as an associate pastor I saw a baffling phenomenon. Certain families in the church would disappear for months on end. We'd call to check on them and they always had plausible explanations for their long absences—traveling, sickness, soccer tournaments, work. Some dropped off the radar never to be heard from again. Others would reappear one Sunday and pick up right where they left off, faithfully attending. I finally got up the nerve to ask one of the guys where he and his wife had been, really. He admitted they'd been having some major marriage problems, so they stopped coming to church because they didn't want anyone to know.

In psychology we have a term for this kind of response to personal problems. It's called *whacked*. Actually, I just decided to call it that. But seriously, avoiding a source of support when things get hard is total self-sabotage. Our old, false self tells us to pull away from the very thing that can help and even strengthen us when we need it most. Shawn Achor, a researcher from Harvard, has done dozens of studies about how people can thrive under stress. He concluded that, "The people who survive stress the best are the ones who actually increase their social investments in the middle of stress, which is the opposite of what most of us do."[4] In study after study, he found social connection trumped all other variables in predicting someone's ability to weather difficult times.

Shame lies and says no one else can understand your struggle. No one understands the addiction. No one is as lonely as you are. No one else has marriage problems. If they find out you have those issues they'll be shocked or judgmental. But that's a lie. Don't believe it. Because if you do, that lie will destroy you and your relationships. It'll keep you stuck behind a wall.

When we believe our struggles are unique, we develop psychological isolation, which eventually leads to physical isolation. We pull away from community out of pride or fear. We believe that no one will truly accept us if they see what happens behind the curtain. It's the same old lie of the false self that says, "Once you are acceptable and get cleaned up you can come to Jesus."

Here's the truth: Jesus will take you just as you are.

And so will healthy community.

Yes, you there in the back. I see your hand. You are about to ask, "Where do we find such community? Because it's not happening with my crew." Well, I'm glad you asked. Healthy community has two key elements. And they are uncomfortable. So you may have to be the brave one who starts modeling it first. If you do, I'm certain others will come around you. You'll find your healthy community. The two elements are transparency and accountability.

THE POWER OF TRANSPARENCY

Back in the day, before all the HD projectors and screens that we use in church to show song lyrics and Bible passages, we used a boxy contraption called a *transparency machine* or an *overhead projector.* We simply wrote the words in black marker on a transparent sheet, then placed it on the machine and the bright light projected it up on the wall. Because it was hand-written, there was no spellcheck. More than a few times I remember the person running the machine licking a finger and erasing a misspelled word right as we were singing it!

Authentic community is a lot like that old machine. Everyone can see our flaws.

I love social media, but it has too much potential for deception. On social media, we can perfectly craft what we show people. We post the picture with our smiling wife at a romantic dinner and never have to show that we were screaming at each other in the car all the way there. When I post a picture of my happy daughter on Facebook, no one knows that it took fifty shots to get that one of her smiling. People regularly comment about how she is always smiling. She smiles a lot, but she does a fair share of crying too.

If you do dare to get transparent on social media, people will tolerate it about 1.3 times. The first time they'll call you courageous and bold. But if you keep being honest about struggles folks will block you: "Sorry, I don't need this negativity in my life, man. You're killing my good vibes." Bottom line: Social media is fun, but it's not a place for true community. It lacks transparency.

Healthy community is transparent. When we project a perfect (but false) image, we never have to really confront the shame-based defenses and habits that limit us. We stay stuck. If you've been hurt then you might be afraid of being transparent. But there's safety that comes when you take the risk, because healthy community has one more key element.

THE NUMBER ONE RULE OF CLIMBING

During my freshman year of college, my roommate came home one day all fired up about rock climbing. He was a pretty impetuous fellow and had gone out and purchased a bunch of climbing gear. He begged me to go climbing with him right after I got home from working an early shift. I was tired, but he wouldn't relent.

"Why can't you just go alone?" I asked.

He shot me an incredulous look. "Dude! Number-one rule of climbing: Never climb alone. Now come on. It'll be fun."

I went, and to my surprise it *was* fun. It wasn't nearly as scary as I thought. Mostly because I learned that wise climbers always use lots and lots of safety gear to help minimize the risk of falling.

And they never climb alone.

Wise climbers are always linked up with another person using protective gear and ropes. They always have someone holding a rope that is connected to an anchor in the wall. They may slip, but they won't fall to their death because they have someone watching out for them, holding the rope.

King Solomon says it this way: "Two are better than one, because they have a good reward for their toil. For if they fall, one will lift up his fellow. But woe to him who is alone when he falls and has not another to lift him up!"[5]

While doing research for this book, I talked to lots of people about community and accountability. I heard lots of personal stories. Some good, some tragic. I found it interesting that folks who had hit rock-bottom through financial ruin, marital infidelity, or moral failure were most vehement about the importance of accountability in community. For every single one of them, the first step in their downward spiral was pulling away from those who knew them well.

A disturbing number of prominent Christian leaders have crashed and burned. Most of them claimed they had accountability, but it was accountability without transparency. I worked with a pastor of a large church for a while. He had strict rules from himself and never made exceptions, even when it created awkward situations. Something he said has stuck with me: "Accountability isn't really accountability unless it's intrusive."

Too often, accountability depends on the person who is being held accountable confessing their struggles to their accountability partner. Problem is, shame and fear of losing what we have often keeps us from confessing. So we hide what's happening, and get caught after it's too late and the situation ruins our lives.

In healthy community people will point out concerns they have about your life. I've heard people say that they felt judged when someone in their community addressed how they were living or a mindset they had.

They said they didn't feel accepted as they were, so they abandoned the community. Nobody likes feeling judged, but there's a fine line between being judged and having someone point out when you are living short of God's best for you.

In healthy community the people around you will love you enough to call you out when you're living short of your true self. They'll say something when they see you in danger. It may feel like you're being judged at times, but that's your false self trying to keep you stuck. Folks may not always confront you in a perfect way, we've all got flaws, but you can't just abandon community when truth hurts. That's self-sabotage. Yes, community is a vulnerable place. It's supposed to be! It's only when others can see and confront our flaws that we can grow.

You need a group of people in your life who have permission to call you out and confront when you are living short of who you really are in Christ. Sure, that's uncomfortable. I know the discomfort well. I've gotten more than a few righteous smack-downs from folks who love me. I don't like having to admit I'm getting a little too proud or controlling. But what's worse is continuing to live short of all God has for me. "Wounds from a friend can be trusted, but an enemy multiplies kisses."[6] Accountability may hurt a little, but it will keep you safe.

If transparency and accountability are the foundation of healthy community, then the bricks and mortar are the spiritual disciplines we practice in community. Just like the spiritual disciplines of meditation, study, and secrecy that we do in solitude, there are disciplines that we do in community. These disciplines allow God to complete his work of making us more like him. Here are a few key practices in community that will help you live out of your true self in Christ.

WORSHIP

Your faith is personal, but it's not just about you and Jesus. "We, though many, are one body in Christ, and individually members one of another."[7]

"Stand on your own!" and "Pull yourself up by your bootstraps!" are not the mindset of a Christian. It's Texan, which I happen to be, which makes community a challenge for me. I want to go it alone. I don't want anyone in my business. But, Christianity is about unity and connection with others. This is why gathering together—in person—with other Christians has to be a priority.

Worship is when we come together, shoulder-to-shoulder, with people of all backgrounds, races, political leanings, and socioeconomic strata, and recognize that God is our source. It's an act of humility. No one is better than anyone else. We're all in need of God. We all need each other on the journey. No matter how successful, strong, weak, or poor we are, God sees us the same: people who are in deep trouble apart from his forgiveness and salvation.

Paul reminds us to, "not neglect our meeting together, as some people do, but encourage one another..."[8] Gathering together is meant to be a source of mutual encouragement. But, when you get a diverse group of people together in church there's bound to be some discomfort. And probably a few things you don't really like. In many ways I can relate to C.S. Lewis when he describes his first experience with church worship:

> *"I disliked very much their hymns, which I considered to be fifth-rate poems set to sixth-rate music. But as I went on I saw the great merit of it. I came up against different people of quite different outlooks and different education, and then gradually my conceit just began peeling off. I realized that the hymns (which were just sixth-rate music) were, nevertheless, be-*

ing sung with devotion and benefit by an old saint in elastic-side boots in the opposite pew, and then you realize that you aren't fit to clean those boots. It gets you out of your solitary conceit."[9]

It's really trendy to downplay the importance of formal church gatherings. I've heard people say, "I love God, I just don't like church." I've even heard people hint that they've grown beyond the need for church. They say their "church" is being with their family or being in the outdoors. I get it. I connect with God on one level in those ways too (that's why I lead outdoor expeditions!), but to say that you've outgrown the need for church borders on arrogance or, as C.S. Lewis calls it, "solitary conceit." (And Heaven knows you don't want to be rebuked by C.S. Lewis!)

We *never* outgrow our need to worship in community. Online church and video sermons are great, but they're not a substitute for gathering together in person. We need to interact with each other, even to irritate each other. It makes us grow and live out the love, patience, kindness and all the other fruits of the Spirit that make up our new identity.

Worshipping together gives us a glimpse of eternity, where we will all stand before God, knowing as we are known[10], and acknowledge that he is God and we need him.

CONFESSION

When we get brave enough to be transparent with our community, we'll realize we aren't alone. When we share our struggles with fear, addiction, temptation, depression, or shame, and hear someone else say, "Me too," it helps us see we don't have to hide. There are others who understand. That's the power of the spiritual discipline of Confession.

"Confess your sins to one another and pray for one another, that you may be healed."[11] We confess to God for forgiveness. We confess to others for healing. I like how Rick Warren describes the power of confession: "If you want to be forgiven, you tell God. If you want to feel forgiven, you've got to tell one other person."[12]

When you know you aren't alone it's a whole lot easier to come out of hiding. Alcoholics Anonymous has saved countless people who lost control of their lives. A lot of the power of the program comes from confession. When alcoholics open up together about their helplessness against alcohol, a support community is formed. No one judges because they're in the same boat. Confessing opens the door to recovery and even makes them stronger.

Confessing the addiction, the affair, or the fear takes courage. It's scary. But the life you really want is always on the other side of your greatest fear. Trust that confession works. Trust that it brings freedom. Make it a regular part of your spiritual disciplines and you'll soon find you've got a lot to celebrate.

CELEBRATION

Celebration is gratitude. It's taking your mind off what's wrong in your life and focusing on all that's right. You may be a long way from where you really want to be, but take a look around and recognize just how far you've come. God has been at work.

I'll admit, I'm not good at this.

I spend most of my mental energy worrying, complaining, and regretting that I'm not as far along in life as I want to be. But living that way leads to discontentment. Gratitude is the antidote for discontentment.

Gratitude is the antidote for discontentment.

When we're grateful for what we have right now it opens our eyes to the good around us. And there's lots of good. You're breathing. You have people who love you. You had enough money to buy this book. (For which I'm very grateful!) Life really is good.

Sure, there's more we want. But we trust that God has a plan for us and we rejoice that we have come this far in that plan. There may be a hard road ahead, but just like he brought us to this point, he'll get us where we need to be. God didn't bring us this far to simply abandon us. When we celebrate, even when things aren't perfect, it's a statement that we have faith in his promises. The best is still ahead because "the path of the righteous is like the light of dawn, which shines brighter and brighter until full day."[13]

Celebration is a learned discipline. We don't just do it when things are good or easy. We do it when things are far from optimal. I saw a great example of this recently when our neighbor took a job in Antarctica. Because of the harsh climate at the South Pole he was required to commit to a year there. Even if he decided halfway through the year that he couldn't handle it, leaving wasn't an option. There are no flights out until the Spring comes again. Unfortunately, he couldn't take his family with him, so he had to leave them in Texas. I loved it when, halfway through his time away, his wife threw a party. They were halfway there. *Woohoo!* Yes, they still had six more months without him, but God had gotten them this far. Celebrate small wins on the journey.

A simple way to start living a life of celebration is to take time to focus on specific things you're grateful for. A few years back a friend of mine recommended I keep a gratitude journal. I took his advice and the results have been so amazing that I highly suggest you do the same. I put one item on the list in the morning. It helps me start the day with gratitude. In the evening I look back and write down what went right that day. And I thank God for it. I end the day with gratitude. You'll be amazed at what it does for your perspective. Some days are harder than others, but if you'll focus on what you're grateful for, celebration will flow out of you.

Celebration is contagious. Celebrate the growth you see in others. Tell your kids when they get it right and use that time as a chance to point out the godly characteristic you see in what they did. Be lavish with kind words and praise. If you see God's work in someone's life, make sure you point it out. Most of the time we are too close to our own lives to see change, so when you see it in others, let them know. Celebrate small victories with those around you.

Another great way to celebrate is to keep visible reminders of what God has done in your life. When God saved Israel from a surprise attack by the Philistines, Samuel "took a stone and set it up…and called its name Ebenezer, saying, 'Thus far the Lord has helped us'"[14] Keep physical reminders of God's faithfulness around you. Keep pictures. Keep simple reminders of hard seasons that God brought you through. One of the physical reminders I keep to remember God's faithfulness is something I got on my flight out of Tibet.

Halfway through that flight from Tibet to Guangzhou, a female flight attendant placed her hand on my shoulder, interrupting my conversation with the inquisitive fellow next to me. She handed me a small bag labeled "THE BAG FOR FORBIDDEN ITEM." She smiled, then walked away. The bag was closed with a red string around a little button. I opened the bag and found the knife that had been confiscated at the checkpoint in Lhasa!

I keep that bag as a reminder of God's faithfulness. Not only did I get my knife back, I was wrapping up a life-changing trip through China with my team. For that I was grateful, and still am today. That bag always reminds me of that trip. It reminds me of the work God did in me on that trip. Find some tangible things you can keep around that remind you of God's faithfulness. He was faithful in the past and he will continue to come through in your life. Celebrate that!

SERIOUS ABOUT COMMUNITY

Like solitude, community won't just happen. It has to become a priority. We're all short on time, and community takes time. It can feel like a lot of work. You'll need to carve time out of your schedule to spend with others. You'll need to be willing to drop the façade and get real. You'll need to risk feeling vulnerable. But if you'll do it, I can guarantee that you'll find a new sense of purpose and calling as you walk with others in the journey to becoming fully you.

THIS IS JUST THE BEGINNING

This is the end of the book, but my prayer for you is that this book will be a new beginning. I pray that you'll embrace the person God says you already are and start living from your true self. You may never go to China. You may never leave a ten-mile radius of your home. But you don't have to. The change can start right where you are. It's an inside job. Get serious about living out of your true self in Christ. Stop hiding behind walls of self-absorption, self-gratification, and control. Don't settle for anxiety, insecurity, anger, and depression as just being part of life. Identify the parts of your false self that are holding you back, then lean into Christ. Give him freedom to do his work through practicing spiritual disciplines.

God is always working. He won't stop until he has freed you up to be all he plans for you. Do your part in that work. Forgive. Seek God in solitude and community. Surrender to God's Spirit. Give him free reign. "And I am sure of this, that he who began a good work in you will bring it to completion at the day of Jesus Christ."[15]

Define yourself as one radically loved by God.
This is your true self, every other identity is an illusion.
— BRENNAN MANNING

REFERENCES

CHAPTER 1 — HIDING THE REAL YOU

1. 2 Cor. 5:17

CHAPTER 2 — THE HURT TRIANGLE

1. Allen, David F. *Contemplation: Intimacy in a Distant World.* Mclean, VA: Curtain Call Productions, LLC. 2004
2. Genesis 2:25, NIV
3. Genesis 3:10, NIV
4. Brown, Brene. *Daring Greatly: How the Courage to Be Vulnerable Transforms the Way We Live, Love, Parent, and Lead.* New York: Avery. (2012)
5. Alexander, Bruce K. "The View from Rat Park." http://www.brucekalexander.com/articles-speeches/rat-park/148-addiction-the-view-from-rat-park Accessed May 8, 2016
6. Proverbs 20:5

CHAPTER 3 — THE GIFT OF ANGER

1. Email conversation with Dr. Curt Elliott, Doctor in China, April 25, 2016
2. Genesis 4:5-7
3. Ephesians 4:26
4. "The Effects of Anger on the Brain and Body." National Forum Journal of Counseling and Addiction. Vol. 2, No. 1, 2013. http://www.nationalforum.com/Electronic%20Journal%20Volumes/Hendricks,%20LaVelle%20The%20Effects%20of%20Anger%20on%20the%20Brain%20and%20Body%20NFJCA%20V2%20N1%202013.pdf
5. Adapted from Allen, David F. *Contemplation: Intimacy in a Distant World.* Mclean, VA: Curtain Call Productions, LLC. 2004.
6. James 1:19

CHAPTER 4 — INTERPRETATION, MISCUES, AND YOUR FAMILY

1. Duhigg, Charles. *The Power of Habit: Why We Do What We Do In Life and Business.* New York: Random House. 2012, 2014. Kindle Version.

2. Ibid., location 124

3. McManus, Erwin. *The Artisan Soul: Crafting Your Life Into a Work of Art.* New York, Harper One. 2014 p73

4. 2 Kings 21:9

5. 2 Kings 23:16, NLT

6. Genesis 50:20

CHAPTER 5 — THE ART OF WAR

1. "What Kind of Game is China Playing" by Keith Johnson, The Wall Street Journal Online, June 11, 2011, Accessed April 15, 2016 http://www.wsj.com/articles/SB10001424052 7023042593045763740135374369 24

2. Romans 7:15,18

3. 2 Corinthians 12:7-9

4. Foster, Richard. *Celebration of Discipline.* London: Hodder and Stoughton. 1989

5. Ephesians 6:12

6. Mark 7:20- 23

7. Marx, K. 1976. *Introduction to A Contribution to the Critique of Hegel's Philosophy of Right.* Collected Works, v. 3. New York. Cited in https://en.wikipedia.org/wiki/Opium_of_ the_people#cite_note-2

8. Matthew 26:52

9. Foster, Richard. *Celebration of Discipline.* London: Hodder and Stoughton. 1989

10. 1 Thessalonians 5:23

11. For more insight on this concept, I highly recommend *The Spiritual Man* by Watchman Nee

12. Tournier, Paul. *The Strong and the Weak.* English Version. Philadelphia: The Westminster Press. 1963. p34

13. Ephesians 2:4-5

14. Romans 5:1

15. 1 John 3:1-3, NLT

16. Welch, Edward T. *Shame Interrupted: How God Lifts the Pain of Worthlessness and Rejection.* New Growth Press. 2012. ebook.

17. Exodus 16:3

18. Lewis, C.S. *The Screwtape Letters, Screwtape Proposes a Toast.* London: Geoffrey Bles: The Centenary Press

19. Galatians 5:22-23

20. Philippians 2:12

21. Lewis, C.S. *Mere Christianity.* New York: MacMillan Pub. Co,. 1952

22. Willard, Dallas. *The Spirit of the Disciplines: Understanding How God Changes Lives.* New York: HarperCollins Publishers. 1990

23. Chesterton, G.K. Taken from "Thoughts" https://www.chesterton.org/

24. Psalm 103:2

25. Philippians 1:6

CHAPTER 6 — THE POWER OF FORGIVENESS

1. Proverbs 4:23

2. "Forgive and Forget" by Tom Valeo. http://www.webmd.com/mental-health/features/forgive-forget Accessed July 12, 2016

3. Worthington, Everett. Professor of psychology at Virginia Commonwealth University and the author of *Forgiveness and Reconciliation: Theory and Applications.* Quoted in https://www.psychologytoday.com/blog/the-squeaky-wheel/201306/the-seven-hidden-dangers-brooding-and-ruminating

4. Luke 22:42

5. Hebrews 5:8

6. Luke 10:37

7. Matthew 18:21-35

8. Mandela, Nelson. *Long Walk to Freedom: The Autobiography of Nelson Mandela.* New York: Little, Brown, and Company. 2008

9. Luke 23:34

CHAPTER 7 — THE STRENGTH IN SOLITUDE

1. Ericsson, Anders and Pool, Robert. *Peak: Secrets from the New Science of Expertise.* New York: Houghton Mifflin Harcourt Publishing Company. 2016

2. "This is Your Brain on Silence." Nautilus Magazine. Daniel Gross. July 7, 2016

3. 1 Kings 19:12

4. Daniel 5:25, Matt. 17:5

5. Foster, Richard. *Celebration of Discipline.* London: Hodder and Stoughton. 1989

6. Philippians 4:6

7. Foster, Richard. *Celebration of Discipline.* London: Hodder and Stoughton. 1989

8. Psalm 1:2-3

9. Psalm 23:6, Romans 8:37, 2 Corinthians 2:14, Philippians 4:19, 2 Corinthians 5:21

10. Isaiah 40:8

11. 1 Samuel 30:16, Psalm 43:5

12. 2 Samuel 6:22

13. Psalm 51:6

14. Psalm 139.23

15. Hebrews 4:12

16. Hebrews 12:1

17. Buechner, Frederick. *Now and Then: A Memoir of Vocation.* New York: HarperCollins Publishers. 1983.

18. Matthew 6:4,18

19. Matthew 8:34

CHAPTER 8 — THE LIFE OF COMMUNITY

1. Matthew 22:37-39
2. 1 John 4:20
3. Bonhoeffer, Dietrich. *Life Together: The Classic Exploration of Christian Community.* New York: Harper Collins. 1954
4. Achor, Shawn as Quoted by Barker, Eric. *Barking Up the Wrong Tree: The Surprising Science Behind Why Everything You Know About Success is (Mostly) Wrong.* New York: Harper One. 2017
5. Ecclesiastes 4:9-10
6. Proverbs 27:6
7. Romans 12:5
8. Hebrews 10:25, NLT
9. Lewis, C.S. *God in the Dock: Essays on Theology and Ethics,* "Answers to questions on Christianity." Grand Rapids: Eerdmans. 1970, p.61-62
10. 1 Corinthians 13:12
11. James 5:16
12. Warren, Rick. Article: "When We Confess We Begin to Heal." http://rickwarren.org/devotional/english/when-we-confess-we-begin-to-heal Accessed 1/19/2016
13. Proverbs 4:18
14. 1 Samuel 7:12, NASB
15. Philippians 1:6

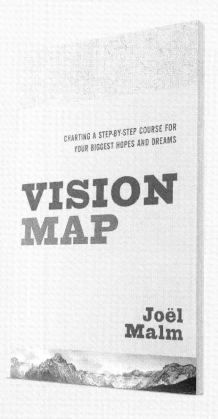

73911808R00107

Made in the USA
Columbia, SC
09 September 2019